"Mike McQueen has written an extr…dinary…CHANGER for parents, teachers, librar…about advocating for what is right for child…the book that lets us all in on the magic t…cessful. This book is chock full of ways to …part of the reading "club," from how to set up a ……onment to how to become a reading role model. Rich with problem solving strategies, and BEST PRACTICES for supporting boys as readers, this book is a valuable resource and indispensable guide to helping all boys become lifelong readers."

~ **Pam Allyn,** Author of *Best Books for Boys: How to Engage Boys in Reading in Ways That Will Change Their Lives*

"Just like we are helping our daughters get more engaged in science and math, we need to pay attention to our sons to make sure they read well and read often. Teacher-Librarian Mike McQueen has some terrific ideas for parents and teachers to get boys to pick up books -- and to keep them reading. His book is an extremely VALUABLE RESOURCE!"

~ **Peg Tyre,** Author of The Trouble with Boys - www.PegTyre.com

"Zest. Knowing Mike McQueen, that's the word that comes to mind. In *Getting Boys to Read*, Mike shares his passion and enthusiasm for engaging boys as readers. Throughout his book, Mike's tips, coupled with thoughtful interviews of other like-minded educators, serve as invitations to the rendezvous called reading. And, what young man doesn't love a rendezvous? Especially one filled with zest!"

~ **Patrick Allen,** Author of *Conferring: The Keystone of Reader's Workshop*

"Mike is an inspiration to us all and his book is a game changer. The QUICK and EASY TO READ format provides parents and teachers with simple yet effective strategies that will make an immediate and positive impact on the boys they want to help. This is a must-read for every educator and parent."

~ **Valerie Braginetz,** Principal and Educational Consultant

"In *Getting Boys to Read*, teacher-librarian, and former reluctant reader, Mike McQueen offers an INSPIRING plea to parents and teachers to do something to help boys who don't love to read. Due to all kinds of home and school factors, too many boys are failing to develop the joy of reading that is one of the essential building blocks for school and lifelong success. IF YOU WANT BOYS TO LOVE READING, *Getting Boys to Read* is the book that will show you how to do it."

~ **Keith Curry Lance,** Library Researcher and Consultant

"I wish I had *Getting Boys to Read* when my sons were in elementary school. I especially loved Tip #60; Let Him Read Comic Books and Tip #65, which talks about utilizing e-readers. All parents who have boys are sure to find something helpful in their quest to help their sons love reading!"
    ~ **Michele Patterson**, President, Jeffco Council PTA

"Mike McQueen's, *Getting Boys to Read* is the most innovative and impressive reading tool available. Mike explains in very simple terms what to do and how to do it. His book provides practical, proven techniques that anyone can implement immediately."
    ~ **Marcia Reece**, Mother, Grandmother, Entrepreneur, and #1 Best-Selling Author of *Marriage Mouse*

"Mike McQueen has walked the walk of frustration, anger, and shame of not being 'a reader.' He knows what it feels like to fail academically – and we are all better off for it. Now, with this book, he brings his first-hand experiences together with hard-won expertise in reading, teaching, and inspiring an active interest in literacy. This means our boys – and those who care about them – now have a manual for how to have success in (and even love) reading. Every year it becomes clearer and clearer – those who read, succeed! Our boys are on the road to success thanks to Mike!"
    ~ **Janet Allison**, Educator, Family Coach, and Author of *Boys Alive! Bring Out Their Best*

"Research shows the three things that stimulate the brain the most are related to survival, novelty, and relevance. All throughout *Getting Boys to Read*, Mike has captured his research and turned it into EASILY IMPLEMENTED STRATEGIES for parents and teachers to engage their boy readers."
    ~ **Dakota Hoyt**, Executive Director of The Gurian Institute (Learning through a Gender Lens)

"*Getting Boys to Read* WILL get boys to read. It is as simple and as important as that! Born from the heart and soul of an award winning teacher-librarian who has made it his life's work to prevent other boys from facing the same struggles he faced when he was a young struggling reader, *Getting Boys to Read* is firmly rooted in common sense, and greatly enhanced with expertise and advice from interviews with more than a dozen other authors. Don't wait to get started!"
    ~ **Judi Herm**, Principal and Educational Consultant, Mindful Consulting, Ltd.

To read many more testimonials and add your own, visit:
www.GettingBoysToRead.com/Testimonials

GETTING BOYS TO READ

Quick Tips for Parents and Teachers

Twenty First Century Publishing
5885 Allison Street, #2223, Arvada, CO 80001

ACKNOWLEDGEMENTS

This book wouldn't exist without the help of many important people...

To my family: my best friend and wife, Jeanne, and my wonderful daughters, Makayla and Seriah; thanks for your love and support during my countless "work- work" nights and author retreats in the RV.

To all guys -- both young and old -- who have struggled with reading; this book is really meant for you!

To my mom, Carol, for getting me out of the slums of Milwaukee and inspiring me to reach for my dreams.

To my sister, Kelly, for reminding me that my story is unique and should be shared with everyone.

To my close friend, Shawn Harris, for your friendship, technical expertise, and skills as a fellow 21st century author.

To my students and colleagues at Lawrence Elementary and McLain High School, thank you for all the great memories and wonderful relationships.

To my teacher-librarian colleagues in Jeffco and across the globe, for your support and kind words of encouragement. Keep fighting the good fight - our kids need you.

To John Hawley, my role model during my teen years, for keeping me out of trouble and inspiring me to attend college.

To Ann Fowler, my high school math teacher, for your big heart and your ability to see my potential.

To Anne Goiran and Deb Hansen, for inspiring me to teach others about getting boys to read.

To the best principals ever: Paula Bradley, Nancy Sommer, Mike Fitzgerald, Judi Herm, Val Braginetz, and Deborah Gard, for molding my career and inspiring me to constantly improve.

To my book coach, Marcia Reece, for your guidance, entrepreneurial advice, and prolific marketing abilities.

To my editors, Stephanie Pellegrino and Kimberly Willahan, thanks for all our last second meetings - both in person and virtually.

To my book designer, Kim Moro, for saving me at the last hour and giving up three weeks of your life to help me prepare this book.

To my web developer and friend Nadeem Shaikh (a.k.a Habib), for your many years of dedicated service.

To my virtual assistant Jenn Tann, for your technical expertise, support, and countless prayers over the years.

To my basketball coaches Chris Schroeder and Wayne Rasmussen, for teaching me how to be a great leader and how to use my skills in a productive way, both on and off the court.

To my Lord and Savior, Jesus Christ, for saving me during college, helping me prioritize what's important in life, and for always being there -- especially during the struggles of making this book.

CONTENTS AT A GLANCE

DETAILED TABLE OF CONTENTS

CHAPTER 2: STRENGTHEN YOUR RELATIONSHIP

CHAPTER 3: CONNECT READING WITH HIS INTERESTS AND NEEDS

CHAPTER 4: LURE HIM WITH THE BEST MATERIALS

CHAPTER 5: MAKE READING INTERACTIVE

CHAPTER 6: MAKE READING FUN

CHAPTER 7: TRY DIFFERENT TECHNIQUES

FOREWORD

I met Mike McQueen after a lecture I was giving in 2009. He explained how excited he was about his blog, *Getting Boys to Read*, and that he was on a mission to help parents and teachers. As we got to know each other during our years together at The Gurian Summer Institute, Mike continued to develop this book. It is inspired by Mike's personal experiences as a struggling reader in combination with his 20-year career as an award-winning teacher-librarian in at-risk schools.

Mike's tips throughout this book are succinct, practical, and useful. As a parent or teacher, you can immediately implement his advice in your classroom and your home. For example, in Tip #8: Do an Extreme Reading Makeover, Mike provides a few very easy steps to follow, with a handful of creative ideas that would surely inspire any boy to read.

The interviews Mike did with other authors and researchers nicely complement his out-of-the-box thinking towards literacy. After reading his interview excerpt with Jim Trelease, author of *The Read Aloud Handbook*, I was inspired to listen to other interviews online. Very impressive!

I hope you will read this book and share it with your friends and colleagues. I believe it will improve the literary lives of the boys you care about.

~ Michael Gurian
Author of *The Minds Of Boys* and *Boys And Girls Learn Differently!*
www.MichaelGurian.com

INTRODUCTION

I ...am...on...a...MISSION - a mission to help boys with reading!

You see, when I was young, I was a poor reader and had a terrible attitude about it - I'm sad to say; I absolutely hated to read. This experience hurt me in all academic areas and even made me miss out on a basketball scholarship.

Despite my academic problems, I made it through high school, graduated from college after five and a half years, and (to the surprise of many) went on to become a successful teacher and award-winning teacher-librarian who now, LOVES TO READ!

I didn't realize it when I was young, but my parents and teachers didn't know some simple, yet very important, things that would have made a huge difference in my overall success as a student. Three burning questions have really bothered me over my 20-year teaching career:

1. Why did I hate reading so much as a young boy?
2. Why didn't the adults in my life help me?
3. What can I do now to help prevent other boys from facing the same struggles?

Inspired by these questions, my mission began in 2006. I started devouring information like a starved lion at an all-you-can-eat steakhouse. I read tons of professional books, articles, and anything else I could get my hands on. I interviewed famous authors, attended professional workshops and worked closely with hundreds of parents, teachers, librarians, and of course, boys.

As my expertise grew, I began traveling all over the United States and Canada, teaching thousands of adults how to help their boys with reading. I also became dedicated to becoming a reading role model myself. I started compiling my knowledge and experience into the "Quick Tips" that are listed in this book.

I have already invested so much time, energy, and money in my mission, the bulk of which have gone toward developing my blog, www.GettingBoysToRead.com My efforts have paid off; my blog has attracted more than a half-million page views.

It's been a very long and difficult road trying to finish this book. Since I teach full-time, I had to steal minutes late at night, during lunch, and at the crack of dawn. I became side-tracked for two years trying to save school libraries from budget cuts. I launched a successful crowdfunding campaign and raised enough money to hire four professional book editors, a book coach (thanks Marcia Reece), two book designers, and numerous virtual assistants. I am ecstatic that the real journey has begun!

Before you get started, study the Contents At A Glance page carefully; the seven chapter titles in this book serve as a chronological blueprint that will help build a strong foundation in the literacy lives of your boys.

I know the tips in this book could have made a big difference in my education growing up. I just hope they help YOU and the boys you work with!

All my best,
Mike

Mike McQueen
Teacher-Librarian, Author, and
Educational Consultant

www.MikeMcQueen.com
www.Facebook.com/AuthorMikeMcQueen
www.Twitter.com/MikeMcQueen
www.GettingBoysToRead.com

My crowdfunding campaign -
www.bit.ly/GettingBoysToRead

CHAPTER 1:

CREATE THE RIGHT ENVIRONMENT

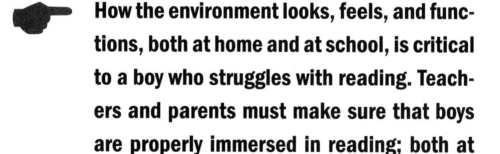 **How the environment looks, feels, and functions, both at home and at school, is critical to a boy who struggles with reading. Teachers and parents must make sure that boys are properly immersed in reading; both at home and at school.**

TIP

1 READ ALOUD DAILY

I have been in education for over 20 years, and almost every elementary teacher I've ever known has stated the best way to help a child succeed in school is to **READ ALOUD EVERY SINGLE DAY**.

Many boys are unorganized, so creating a structured and consistent reading environment will help them thrive. When read aloud time is scheduled and enforced, on a regular basis, they will know it's a mandatory activity, and should resist less – especially if the process becomes a fun routine.

If you have fallen off-track, it's never too late to start; if needed, use this book as an excuse to start a routine.

If you want further inspiration, listen to my audio interview with the famous, Jim Trelease, author of *The Read Aloud Handbook* (over two million copies sold):

www.GettingBoysToRead.com/JimTrelease

PARENTS:

Shortly after our children were born, my wife and I implemented a bedtime routine suggested from the book, *Seven O'clock Bedtime* by Inda Schaenen. We scheduled bath time promptly at 6:30 PM, immediately followed by the most important time of the day – read aloud.

Avoid these excuses:

- I'm too tired after a long day of work
- I'm not that good at reading
- I can't find something my son likes to read

TEACHERS:

Read aloud time at school may be the only chance he has to experience a book with an adult, especially if his parents are not reading with him at home. Make time in your busy schedule.

TIP

2 RECRUIT MALE ROLE MODELS

An alarming number of boys lack positive male role models in their daily lives who can set a good example for reading. When you consider how few male elementary teachers there are (about 10%), it's no wonder why so many boys struggle or disengage with reading.

Part of my lifelong goal is to be a reading role model for all kids. I've created a variety of inspirational videos – some relate to reading and others give advice for various things in life. Just point him to: www.MikeMcQueen.com/Videos

PARENTS:

Keep your eyes open for positive men amongst your family, friends, or neighborhood and reach out to them for help. Be persistent - the more you ask, the more likely they will be willing to serve as role models. When you do find a potential volunteer, follow these tips:

- Make a plea for how much your son needs a reading role model
- If needed, alleviate potential anxiety by suggesting a variety of reading materials (books, magazines, comics, web sites, graphic novels, etc)
- Suggest for him to take your son to a library or bookstore, your treat of course

TEACHERS:

Talk with your principal and/or librarian and schedule male author visits. Flood your classroom throughout the year with older boys from high school or college who will give a pep talk about how reading has improved their lives. Primary and intermediate teachers should team up together and run a "Study Buddy" program. An effective study buddy program builds a culture of literacy and a great sense of community throughout the entire school.

TIP

3 LET HIM BE OBSESSED

It is very common for boys to become obsessed with a hobby or recent interest. If his obsession carries over into his reading habits, be thankful and don't get frustrated if he wants to keep reading the same thing over and over again. While it's important to provide new reading opportunities, it must be done with a gentle, inviting approach so you don't extinguish his reading flame. Feed his fire with your support.

Quite often, boys will get hooked on one specific book or topic and then read it OVER AND OVER again, especially when they are younger. Often, with the best intentions, parents or teachers try to convince him to branch out and try something new or more challenging.

Don't pressure him to abandon something he loves. Instead, encourage him to continue reading!

Let him read it over and over again if he wants to; this repetitive process stimulates his reading needs. Perhaps he missed things in the text or just LOVES it so much he wants to feel the experience again. Have faith he will satisfy his obsession once his needs are met. If you pressure him to move on before he is ready -- you may risk isolating yourself and, even worse, turning him off to reading.

TIP

4 | KNOW WHEN TO BACK OFF

Too often, well-intended parents or teachers become so worried about improving a boy's reading skills they become forceful, pushing him on their schedule rather than his own. Our goal should be to **IMMERSE** boys in reading daily – not submerge them. Immersion can be tricky because it takes balance.

We can't disengage too much or he will fall through the cracks. On the other hand, we can't push him too hard or he will shut down and his attitude will plummet. Proper immersion includes surrounding him with reading throughout each day, but in a way that he perceives as positive and useful.

When he needs a break, recognize it and tell him you're willing to give him a day off every once in a while. Remind him that you are not giving up, that reading must become a part of his daily life, and he will pick up again with the routine the next day.

Start Him Off Right

His reading experience during the first five years of life will impact his entire future. During this vital time he should establish a love of reading and a strong foundation of basic skills, so when he is ready to read he is properly equipped. His problem is that he can't prepare himself without your help.

PARENTS

Your task to start him off right is critically important, but really quite simple:

Make reading a fun and enjoyable experience

every single day from the moment he is born. If you read aloud and discuss a variety of books every day for 15 minutes he will be properly prepared when the time comes to learn how to read.

TEACHERS:

Make sure parents get the inspiration and education they need, especially in at-risk neighborhoods. Don't wait until parents have kids who are old enough to start school – reach out to the community of parents with newborns, so they can start positive routines from day one. Host a few "Parent Literacy" nights and properly market your events so parents are aware. At the events, pass out information to help them learn about specific things they should be doing.

TIP # 6 DON'T LET HIM BECOME A SCREEN ZOMBIE

BEFORE

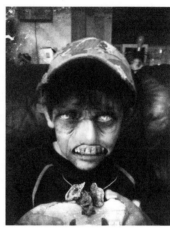

AFTER

Video games, cell phones, and televisions are the three biggest culprits responsible for hypnotizing boys into becoming screen zombies. These devices are time thieves, robbing them from many opportunities to read. A boy's most popular excuse for not reading is, "I don't have time."

Don't accept that lame excuse – turn off the power and plug him into a book.

PARENTS:

SET BOUNDARIES for screen time. Remind your son these devices are a privilege and enforce restrictions when they become an obsession. Addressing the issue is worth the battle, no matter how much he whines or complains.

TEACHERS:

Your responsibility is to educate both your boys and their parents about the problems with too much screen time. Have on-going conversations and send home reminders; encourage parents to stand up to this epidemic. Make sure parents read the tip above.

GET DAD INVOLVED

Author Daniel Hall (www.DanielHallPresents.com) and his son.

How often a boy sees his dad read, or not read, will have an enormous impact on him. Most dads need guidance and constant reminders to read and discuss books with their sons. Many dads are inexperienced readers themselves and are not used to taking this leadership role. Be persistent in getting dad involved with his son's reading journey. You will do wonders and they both need you.

Use these tips to set male role models up for success:

- **Empathize** with him if struggles with reading. Tell him that his low skills are okay, because modeling and a positive attitude are most important.
- **Encourage** him that his son will mimic his attitude and habits about reading. Convince him that by trying, he will send the message that his son should try too. Compliment them both - often.
- **Clarify** what counts as reading. (For more ideas, see my other tip, "Expand the Definition of Reading.")
- **Remind** him to TALK to his son constantly about the things they are both reading.
- **Require** him to schedule a consistent routine.
- **Suggest** shorter pieces of text: magazines, how-to books, and web-site articles are great.
- **Teach** him how to find good reading materials on topics that they both like.
- Take photos of them reading together.
- If there is no 'dad' at home, refer to my other tip, "Recruit Male Role Models."

TIP

8 DO AN EXTREME READING MAKEOVER

The goal of an extreme reading makeover is to change his immediate surroundings at home or at school to a shockingly new, exciting, reader-friendly, and kid-created space. Engage him from the very beginning with the makeover to get his buy-in and a sense of ownership.

Steps:

1. explain the goal: to make the space look and feel "cool"
2. connect the space to reading
3. create a sense of ownership
4. analyze the problems of the space
5. ask questions
6. research ideas
7. make a plan
8. kick butt to execute the makeover

Possible components include:

- cool reading furniture: lamp, end table, bean bag, chair, rug, etc.
- reading fort
- magazine rack
- eBook reading area
- huge photos or painted mural
- hidden compartment for a special diary or book

- fancy handmade artwork
- black lights, and/or
- a refrigerator

Complete the makeover one project at a time. As needed, recruit family members or other volunteers to help. As the makeover starts to take shape, he should develop a sense of pride and improved attitude towards his reading environment.

To see photos and learn about the extreme reading makeovers I have done, visit:

www.GettingBoysToRead.com/ExtremeReadingMakeovers

9 CREATE A READING PHOTO WALL

What better way for a boy to see himself as a reader than to literally see himself reading? Photos are a permanent reminder, and are great for his reading self-esteem.

PARENTS:

Adapt the teacher tip below to suit your needs at home. Displaying framed photos of him with books or magazines can make a great impact.

TEACHERS:

Have your students take photos of each other reading their favorite materials. Explain the goal to combine reading, technology, and photography. Have them shoot, print, and display photos throughout the year on a bulletin board. Tap into family literacy by encouraging them to bring photos of themselves reading at home with family members. Let them add fun, creative captions and the photo wall will take on a life of its own as it grows throughout the year. Encourage photos from the library, book store, comic shop, or wherever!

TIP

10   HAVE HIM GET TO KNOW ME

I take pride in being a fun, positive male role model. I'm passionate to help kids avoid the struggles I have gone through. Have him watch my videos on book reviews, advice, and reading tips. If possible, hire me to speak at his school or conduct a one-on-one video Skype with me. Contact me with details of your needs by visiting: www.MikeMcQueen.com

TIP #

11

SET UP A "BOOKS FOR BOYS" DISPLAY (TEACHERS)

Recruit a few boys and inform them you need help inspiring other boys to read. Explain the goal is to acknowledge that boys and girls often have different tastes in reading. Start with a brief brainstorm session and make a list of hobbies other guys may be interested in reading about. Guide them to related reading materials, work with them on creating the bulletin board, and collaborate on a plan for advertising the display to other boys. Make a big deal out of the process, no matter how much (or little) they help. You want this to be a positive, memorable experience. If needed, recruit a group of girls to make a "Books for Girls" display and make it a fun competition.

TIP # 12

ENTICE HIM WITH FOOD

Look for opportunities to connect reading with food. Most boys, especially older boys, get very excited about something if there is any chance food is involved. This doesn't mean it has to be unhealthy food or a huge feast. For the best effect, wait until he's really hungry.

TIP # 13

HELP HIM AVOID AUDITORY OVERLOAD

A boy's brain is not wired to handle a lot of auditory information. During his day, he is bombarded with an on-going requirement to listen; teachers, parents, and other adults demand his attention. Once his senses are overwhelmed he will likely become fidgety, frustrated, zoned out, or otherwise disengaged. Prepare his brain for reading by avoiding over-stimulation of his senses, especially his sense of sound. If he becomes over-stimulated, give him a quick brain break and have him move for a few minutes.

THINK ALOUD

Teacher Stephanie Pellegrino

Boys need to hear you model your thought process before, during, and after you read. What pops into your head? What questions, concerns, problems, ideas, likes, or dislikes do you have when you read? Boys often lack these skills, no matter what age they are.

Have **HIM** do "Think Alouds" as well. As he learns from watching you, he'll start developing a skill that will last him a lifetime.

TIP

15

CLUTTER A SMALL TABLE (PARENTS)

Look at this photo of my living room table. Notice the assortment of different reading materials from each member of my family. Sometimes this table is neatly organized, but most often it's a cluttered mess with a variety of reading materials scattered in every direction. This "messy look" is often better because it sets a casual and inviting tone -- a reminder that reading isn't sterile and uniform. It also sends a message that reading is an ACTIVE part of our family's daily living space.

TIP

16 HELP HIM FIND REASONS TO READ

Teach him that reading can answer his questions and solve his personal wants and needs. The more often he sees reading as meaningful and useful, the more often he'll want to invest his time and energy towards it.

8 Good Reasons for a Boy to Read:

1. learn or improve a skill
2. solve a problem
3. accomplish a goal
4. fill a curiosity
5. gain power
6. laugh
7. get scared
8. escape reality

TIP

17 TAKE A TEAM APPROACH

Teacher Lisa Hughes

Why put the pressure all on yourself to help boys with reading? Think about all of the possible resources available at your fingertips: other teachers or parents, librarians, administrators, reading specialists, instructional coaches, counselors, paraprofessionals, and more.

One of my colleagues, Lisa Hughes (in the photo above), is one of the best teachers I have ever worked with. Even her elite level of expertise didn't stop her from reaching out to me for help with her small group of boys.

It only took us 20 minutes or so to collect a pile of great, relevant books for her group, based on topics they listed on note cards (another great tip). That planning, along with my short "book talk," helped her boys feel special, and consequently inspired them to read.

It's up to you to reach out for help.

TIP

18

ENCOURAGE NONFICTION...

In my experience, most boys prefer nonfiction. Nonfiction gives many boys a purpose to read, especially when it is relevant to something personal. The National Common Core Standards have done a great job addressing the need to implement more nonfiction into curricula. A truly balanced approach to literacy will expose boys to EQUAL portions of nonfiction and fiction.

TIP

19

PROVIDE COMFY SEATING

Comfortable seating is possibly the most important criteria for a space to attract practically all kids, especially teenage readers. There are many affordable seats to entice boys to read - beanbags, couches, gamer "rocker" chairs, patio swings, leather office chairs, hammocks, etc. As adults, we read in a variety of relaxed, comfortable arrangements. Why force our boys to read while sitting up straight in hardwood chairs? Have him select a seat he finds most comfortable for reading.

TIP # 20

SCHEDULE MALE AUTHOR VISITS

Author Todd Parr - www.ToddParr.com

When a boy meets an author and hears his success story, it provides an opportunity for the boy to connect reading with success. Author visits allow for role modeling and can also connect to writing, which makes for a great literacy experience. Kids often connect with authors of the same gender, so be sure to schedule as many male authors as possible.

TIP

21   RECRUIT GRANDPARENTS

Author and entrepreneur Marcia Reece - www.MarciaReece.com

Grandparents are the best! They know how important reading is and will often do whatever they can to play a role in the education of their beloved grandchildren. Take advantage of their expertise, availability, and willingness to help. Schedule an on-going reading routine and encourage them to do reading-related activities with their grandkids. Have them watch my "Partner Reading" video: www.GettingBoysToRead.com/PartnerReading

Interview with Stephen Krashen, Author of The Power of Reading: Insights from the Research

Stephen Krashen - www.sdKrashen.com

Below is a short excerpt from our interview where Mr. Krashen discusses the reading environment.

MIKE MCQUEEN:

Let's talk about poverty and the impact that it has on struggling readers. As parents and educators, what can we do?

STEPHEN KRASHEN:

The first thing to do – not the only thing to do, but the first thing to do – is to guarantee access to books. This means libraries. Let me tell you a little bit of what we know about libraries. This is very exciting research because it points to real solutions for a modest amount of money put in the right places.

We know, first of all, when children have access to books, they read more. Now the critics say this isn't true - that kids will just sit around; they won't look at books, etc. No, that's not true … when children have access to books that are comprehensible and interesting, they do read them; just about every child reads them.

I've just finished a paper looking at research on Sustained Silent Reading programs and whether students are engaged or not, and the only times you see students who are not engaged -- other than maybe one or two here and there -- are when the books aren't available; the books aren't any good; or when the teachers make them sit alert in their seat and pay attention every minute, where it's kind of like being in prison; or make them do extensive reports.

When you do it right, kids can and do read - if they have interesting stuff to read. I mean, look at the influence of *Twilight* and *Harry Potter*; how many kids read these books and really like them? And R.L Stine, who I think has done more for literacy than just about anybody else. For my generation, my son's generation, and my daughter's generation it was Stan Lee, Marvel Comics, and Archie; [they created] a generation of readers who've done very, very well. So when you provide access to books, kids will read them, if [the books are] interesting and comprehensible.

Number Two: If they read a lot, they get more literate. The overwhelming evidence behind free, voluntary reading -- I am more impressed with it all the time. Those who read more, of course they read better, they write better, they are more likely to have acceptable writing style; their vocabulary is better, their spelling is better – not always perfect but really good. Their grammar is better; that means they have better control of complex grammatical structures.

Not only that, they know more. Study after study shows this. Keith Stanovich has done a very, very good series of studies on this. People who read a lot know more about everything; of course, literature, science and all of this, but they also know more about practical matters. Colleagues of mine and I just published a paper called, "Are Readers Nerds?" and the answer is no. They are more involved with the world - young people and adults. They are more likely considered to be interesting people. Reading just wins all around and the answer is making sure that these books are available.

To listen to our entire interview, visit:

www.GettingBoysToRead.com/StephenKrashen

CHAPTER 2:

STRENGTHEN YOUR RELATIONSHIP

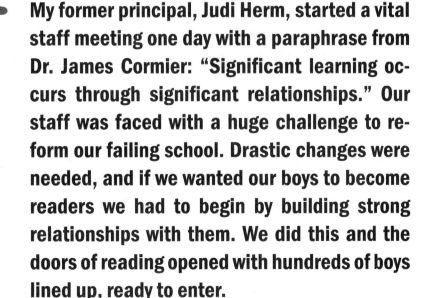

My former principal, Judi Herm, started a vital staff meeting one day with a paraphrase from Dr. James Cormier: "Significant learning occurs through significant relationships." Our staff was faced with a huge challenge to reform our failing school. Drastic changes were needed, and if we wanted our boys to become readers we had to begin by building strong relationships with them. We did this and the doors of reading opened with hundreds of boys lined up, ready to enter.

TIP
22 | SCHEDULE ONE-ON-ONE TIME

When you set aside one-on-one time, you send a message that he is special and that you care about him. Your time together should be fun and meaningful. Set a goal to first connect with him on a friendly, personal level. Get to know each other -- talk, play a game, do a few things he enjoys. After you bond, even a little bit, it will be much easier to integrate reading into your relationship. Schedule reoccurring get-togethers to keep your connection strong.

TIP
23

LOAD YOUR DESK WITH COOL GADGETS (TEACHERS)

Mr. McQueen

Sometimes a boy needs an excuse to come and chat with you without looking like a teacher's pet. These cool gadgets on my desk spark curiosity and entice guys to approach me. This opens the door for conversation, which leads to a relationship, and may open a door to help him in the future.

TIP # 24
WRITE HIM A QUICK NOTE

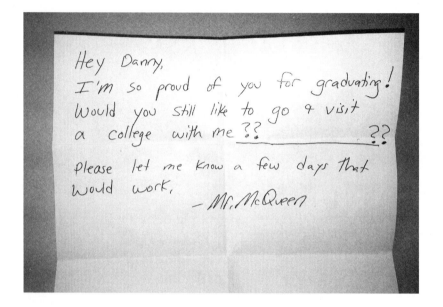

Hey Danny,
I'm so proud of you for graduating!
Would you still like to go & visit
a college with me ??   ??

Please let me know a few days that
would work,
— Mr. McQueen

Every once in a while, set aside 60 seconds and jot down a personalized, handwritten note on a small, folded-up piece of paper. Give him a compliment, then ask a question and leave a space for his reply. Writing a personalized, printed message not only shows that you care, it also teaches him that reading and writing is a great tool for communication.

TIP
25
HAVE ONGOING CONVERSATIONS

Teacher-Librarian Andi Johnson

There is plenty of research about how important language development is, especially with younger boys. Talk with him about anything and everything. Ask him what he liked or didn't like about what he read. Ask him questions, questions, and more questions! The more you engage him in reading conversations the better. Also, be a good listener.

TIP #

26 INVITE HIM TO LUNCH (TEACHERS)

How often are the "naughty" boys invited to lunch? Hardly ever! These boys are almost always the ones who struggle the most with reading. By having lunch with him in the classroom (or cafeteria), you

---

Send the message that you care and that he matters.

During lunch together, engage in a fun conversation and make him feel comfortable. Slip in a quick talk about a cool book, but make sure the conversation does not feel like a school assignment.

You don't have to do this all the time and you might be surprised how much one visit will impact him.

TIP

27   GET TO THE SOURCE OF HIS PROBLEM

Don't assume you know exactly what his reading problem is. What appears on the surface could be disguising deeper issues. If he has a bad attitude, there are a few logical reasons and you must find out all the possible factors.

Maybe he is struggling with a big personal problem or situation at home or school. Perhaps he has some kind of hidden disability that has not yet been uncovered. If needed, team up with a professional to help diagnose and treat whatever concerns may be present. Parents and teachers must work closely together with the boy. Lines of communication must be open amongst everyone.

> *Get a good understanding about his past and present reading experiences.*

TIP

28 Make A Positive Phone Call

A boy loves to know that his parents and teachers have had a positive conversation about his reading attitude or progress. Look for any simple excuse to make the call.

A phone call is a personal, meaningful, "win-win-win" situation for everyone - the teacher, parent, and the boy.

Example:

"Dear _____, I just wanted to make a quick phone call to let you know I appreciate your efforts with Billy and to share something great today that he did with reading. I thought you would appreciate knowing what happened… "

TIP
29 PLAY OUTSIDE WITH HIM

I t's rare to see a teacher or parent play outside with a group of boys, especially older ones. Whether it's at school during recess or at home in his backyard, when a boy sees an adult in HIS domain, he is almost always excited and grateful. When you play outside with him, you humble yourself, gain his respect, and allow a great opportunity for him to trust and admire you. Once this occurs, you can get him in the right frame of mind to discuss reading.

TIP
30 · MANAGE HIS BEHAVIOR

Your goal of inspiring him to read will be more difficult if his behavior is out of control and/or he doesn't respect you.

Take him aside and in a brief, respectful conversion, tell him you:

- care
- want to help, and
- are willing to work together to find a resolution

Take ownership for his behavioral problems. Ask friends or colleagues for suggestions. As his behavior improves, his chances for reading successes increase.

TIP

31 | BUILD HIS CONFIDENCE

When I became a homeowner, my attitude and skill level for household repairs stunk. Each time I encountered a new problem, my wonderful family smothered me with compliments, praise, and words of encouragement. Their efforts helped me believe in myself as a "handyman." As my confidence grew, I became less intimidated to tackle harder problems. I eventually developed a better attitude, became quite handy, and saved our family piles of money. This same concept can be applied to helping boys with reading.

Improve his reading confidence and inspire him through your

COMPLIMENTS, PRAISE, and ENCOURAGEMENT.

The more often you do this, the more rapidly his attitude and skill level will improve.

TIP #

32 VERBALIZE ALL SUCCESSES

H e needs to constantly hear you say encouraging things to him as he engages with reading.

Was he finally able to find a book that he liked?

- Ask him how he found it and then describe how impressed you are with his skills.

Did you catch him reading something online?

- Explain how that is a great way to read.

Did he tell you about something that he read and liked or disliked?

- Thank him for sharing.

Keep your eyes open. There are opportunities waiting around every corner to say nice things to him about reading. Your positive re-enforcement will only make him grow as a reader.

TIP # 33

CONNECT TO HIS STRENGTHS

Every boy has a skill or strength that you can use to his advantage. Don't forget that it's very important for him to appear strong and knowledgeable.

Ask him questions and show excitement with his replies. Make reading more meaningful by helping him connect his strengths to reading materials, especially nonfiction.

Draw lots of attention to his strengths and areas of expertise!

34 SET HIM UP TO SUCCEED

Teacher-Librarian Donna Ostwald

Far too often boys are forced into reading situations that doom them to fail. Don't make him read things that are frustratingly difficult, boring, or overwhelming.

Incremental successes lead to readers who become self-confident risk-takers.

If you want him to be confident as a reader, make sure you know his abilities, stamina, interests, and limitations.

TIP # 35

ALLOW EASY READING

In today's day and age, there is way too much academic pressure for kids to improve their reading skills. Focused, directed reading is important for growth, but in a world obsessed with test preparation, many boys become negative and burnt out by these intense reading requirements.

Give him plenty of opportunities to read for pleasure

As adults, very few of us find pleasure in constantly being challenged to decode or comprehend.

We want to read for pleasure, to curl up on the beach with a great novel, or smile after a book teaches us how to build a tree house. We want our reading experience to be fun and easy without a high-stakes test to follow.

TIP
36

GIVE HIGH-FIVES

It doesn't matter how young or old he is, or how cool he tries to act - getting a high-five always feels great after accomplishing something. A high-five gives him public recognition, a sense of power, and a chemical release of energy, which fills his biological need for physical contact. Keep your eyes open for reading-related opportunities to give high-fives. The more you give, the better.

TIP
37 GIVE ELECTRIC KNUCKLES

High fives are great, but another alternative to acknowledge success is a manly fist-to-fist collision commonly known as a "Fist Bump." Step it up a notch and teach him my corny invention, "Electric Knuckles." Once both knuckles touch, make a "zzzzz" sound indicating electric sparks just flew (dramatic acting helps). The goal of Electric Knuckles is to make him smile or roll his eyes, with bonus points for both. Electric Knuckles build his confidence by complimenting him in a fun, silly, and memorable way.

TIP

38 DON'T SHOVE IT DOWN HIS THROAT

I n your good-hearted mission to get him to become a reader, be careful not to suffocate him.

If you give him too much to read or get on his case too often, he will likely give up and disconnect even more - the OPPOSITE of what you were intending to do.

Gauge his tolerance.

Give him text he is comfortable with, and ease him in at a pace that **HE CAN HANDLE**.

TIP # 39

DO KIND GESTURES

In a desperate plea to brainwash me into liking country music, my good friend, Mark bought me this three-volume collection by famous country musician, Tim McGraw.

Mark's approach was sound:

- He gave it to me as a gift. This made me feel great and tempted me to listen.
- He picked an album that was popular with a lot of guys.
- Most importantly, he picked a country musician that he thought I WOULD LIKE.

I was touched by his kind gesture and had every intention to listen to his gift, despite my disinterest in country music. My problem, though, was that 47 songs were way too **OVERWHELMING** and his gracious gift sat on my desk, untouched for months.

I explained to him one day that it was too much for me and that he needed to narrow it down to something I could handle and succeed with (fortunately, I knew my limitations). I suggested picking only the three songs that I would like the most. He skimmed the titles and gave me this paper:

Once Mark narrowed my choices, it helped me feel less over-whelmed in the music he was suggesting. I thought, "I think I can handle only three songs, even though country music 'isn't my thing.'"

Despite all that progress, I was STILL dragging my feet to do my "assignment" and listen to these personalized songs, much like a resistant boy reader. In my mind, I still secretly doubted I'd like his songs and still contemplated whether I should invest my time to listen. I needed another nudge. To my surprise, I received this simple text message from Mark the next day, which changed everything:

Mark's follow-up text message was the vital nudge that inspired me to listen to his suggested songs, which ultimately improved my attitude toward country music.

My story with Mark is similar to encouraging boys to read:

- Do kind gestures that involve reading
- Don't overwhelm him
- Pick three things that HE WILL LIKELY ENJOY
- Follow up with a gentle nudge

TIP # 40
NEVER LET HIM APPEAR WEAK

As boys get older, many mistakingly associate reading as a "girl thing" and fear that if they are seen reading, it will make them look less masculine.

If there is the slightest chance he thinks he will look weak amongst his peers, he will disengage faster than you can blink. His perceived reputation influences his mindset, opinions, and actions – especially as he approaches his teen years. It's easier for him to say, "reading sucks" or "I hate reading" than to admit his insecurities or incompetence.

If you hear someone tease him about reading, speak up and defend him! Even better, teach him to defend himself. Warn him that he might encounter "razzing," but despite that, reading is still manly. Remind him that strong, famous, and successful men read everyday to solve problems and make things easier for themselves. Stifle any negative peer pressure he may be worrying about by giving him the tools he needs to defend himself with his peers.

INTERVIEW

Interview with Jim Trelease, Author of The Read Aloud Handbook

Jim Trelease - www.Trelease-On-Reading.com

Below, Mr. Trelease discusses reading aloud and relationships.

MIKE MCQUEEN:

What connections are there between reading aloud and relationships?

JIM TRELEASE:

Things surface within a story that are intimate, that are personal, especially with fiction as opposed to nonfiction. With fiction you are crawling inside not just the plot, but you are crawling into the soul of the being of the individuals in the story and you are seeing how they think and how they act in response to how they think. It is basically for the pickings of the human condition.

It is exactly what football coaches do with the team on Monday morning after a game. They take the game films and they run them for the team. And they run them in slow motion. And then they run them backwards and forwards, and again and again, and what they are breaking down is to see how that individual player on their team and the opposing team behaved.

In a novel, as you read it, you are running the game film of life for that child; he is seeing that character encounter a situation. The character is thinking through the situation, making a decision, and acting in a certain way for better or for worse -- but the child is seeing it in slow motion.

Then, you follow the characters through the rest of the story as they live with either the benefits or the non-benefits of how they behave. It's a very personal thing, and yet it's being shared aloud by the reader and the child, so you're both experiencing this together.

When it's a one-on-one situation – a father or mother and child as opposed to the whole family – there are added benefits because there may be things that come up in the story that they might not talk about in front of the rest of the family [or class]. But, when it's one-on-one they'll say, "I had that happen to me one time; I was out on the playground..." and then they start to tell you something that they would not have otherwise shared.

I did a workshop for a group of teachers at an institution

for disturbed children. These were deeply disturbed children. These were children who were so disturbed that they had to be removed from the home. It was a group therapy situation, live-in residents, and there are about 20 kids to each cottage. Sadly, nobody had ever explored the idea of bibliotherapy with any of these kids. I went in and did a little workshop on it, and then they invited me back about two months later for dinner with the kids and staff. Afterwards, when it was just the counselors and me, they regaled me with stories of the kids who opened up. It wasn't a one-on-one situation because they were doing a group reading -- they had 15-20 kids in the cottage and they were reading *James and the Giant Peach* by Roald Dahl. Kids were basically talking about their own feelings, but they were using James instead of themselves, so they could describe James and how he must have been feeling -- his anger at situations -- but they were basically talking about themselves; they were able to use James as a substitute for themselves. So there's potential for a great bond to exist between the reader and the listener when you read aloud.

To listen to our entire interview, visit:
www.GettingBoysToRead.com/JimTrelease

Interview with Donalyn Miller, Author of The Book Whisperer

Donalyn Miller - *www.BookWhisperer.com*

Below, Ms. Miller discusses the role of confidence in struggling readers.

MIKE MCQUEEN:

What role does confidence play with kids who are struggling readers?

DONALYN MILLER:

A lot of kids -- this could apply to any grade level -- just don't have enough experience as independent readers to feel confident. They haven't read many books; they seemingly don't have experience in understanding how to find authors they might like or relate to.

Even if you took them to the library or to a bookstore, they might be intimidated by that activity because they don't really know how to pick books for themselves. My first suggestion for those kids would be to help them find just one or two great books they could finish on their own or with a parent -- maybe books by authors who are prolific, like Gary Paulsen. We talk about him a lot in upper elementary and middle school; he's written many books for kids and they're consistently good and appeal to a wide number of readers. If you could get a kid to read one book by Gary Paulsen, then you potentially have exposed him to about a hundred other books he may enjoy. Gordon Korman is another author who is very prolific and quite popular with kids.

With kids who don't possess reading confidence, I will try to pick one book I know to be consistently popular – it might not be popular with every child, but it seems to appeal to a lot of children.

Read that book with him or give it to him and then use it as an in-road for more books, so that he is less intimidated when he visits the library; familiarity with a couple of authors may give him the confidence he needs to independently explore. He may not know many authors, but now he'll know one or two.

He may not feel like he could read long books, which are often intimidating, but he could read a few shorter ones perhaps. Baby steps are important when slowly building confidence; readers build their confidence through reading. Reading a book, teaching him, and sharing great reading experiences can help him get those stepping-stone books and reading experiences that lead him towards more confidence and efficacy as a reader.

To listen to our entire interview, visit:

www.GettingBoysToRead.com/DonalynMiller

CHAPTER 3:

CONNECT READING WITH HIS INTERESTS AND NEEDS

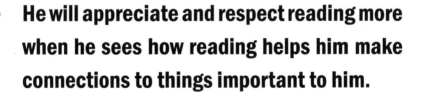

He will appreciate and respect reading more when he sees how reading helps him make connections to things important to him.

RESPECT HIS PASSIONS

As adults, it's important that we don't let our own reading preferences or biases have a negative impact on the boys who we are trying to help. If we make him feel badly about the things he likes to read, he will disengage as a reader. I have witnessed both parents and teachers say these damaging statements:

- "Put that book back and get a 'real' book"
- "That is too easy for you to read; you need to challenge yourself more."
- "That book is too hard for you. Stop pretending to read it."
- "You're reading that same exact thing AGAIN?!"

Even a little, well-intended "razzing" can damage his attitude towards reading. Don't make fun of what he chooses to read or how poorly he reads, or complain if the material is boring to you or not challenging enough for him.

TIP # 42

Empower Him By Letting Him Choose

Most boys have a natural desire for power and control. If a boy is constantly required to read things an adult chooses, how will this eventually make him feel? Incapable? Frustrated? Discouraged? Resentful? POWERLESS? The more often he gets to self-select his reading materials, the more likely he will develop a sense of ownership, positive self-image, and POWER. This is true at school and especially at home.

PARENTS:

Remember your responsibility should be to help him have a fun, on-going, and positive reading experience at home. Here are a few tips for a great experience:

- Never force him to read a book just because you liked it when you were a kid.
- Don't play the role of a reading teacher - let his teacher focus on improving his skills while you focus on improving his desire.
- When you read aloud together, it's better when you accommodate his reading preferences 90% of the time, even if you don't like his choices or are tired of the same thing over and over.

- If you are helping him learn how to read, make sure to closely follow the same reading strategies his teacher uses.
- Avoid overusing the "sound it out" technique.
- When he reads independently at home, ALWAYS give him a chance to select the materials he wants.

TEACHERS:

Make reading a give-and-take relationship. Look for short, bite-sized texts that teach the skill or concept without taking forever to read. Library visits should always include the opportunity to get a book of his choice.

TIP # 43

STAY UPDATED WITH HIS INTERESTS

A few times a year, have a positive, private conversation about his recent interests and hobbies. Discuss what he is interested in, anything that he has read lately, what reading formats he prefers, and what his recent attitude towards reading is.

Jot down a few notes and then schedule time to take action and help him find reading materials connected to his interests.

PARENTS:

A great alternative to a written survey is to play, "The Question Game," when you simply take turns asking and answering questions on any topic that comes to mind.

TEACHERS:

If you use written surveys, the shorter and easier the surveys are, the better. Tell him to answer the questions to the best of his ability and not worry about spelling or grammar.

TIP # 44

TEACH HIM ABOUT NONFICTION

Nonfiction serves a great purpose for many boys – it often fills an interest they have and gives them a purpose to read.

Teach him:

- how to use the table of contents and index to quickly find information
- how to quickly skim a nonfiction book to determine if it meets his needs
- how to use different text features to navigate and comprehend information as he reads (diagrams, headings, captions, charts, etc)
- that good images and captions will pull him into the text
- it's okay to read only the parts he needs or wants; this is a common reading strategy with nonfiction readers
- see Tip 53: Let Him Know That It's Okay To Leave A Nonfiction Book Unfinished

TIP # 45

GUIDE HIS DESIRE FOR VIOLENCE

Boys are naturally drawn to violent topics such as weapons, horror, blood, war, fighting, and hunting. When you ban these topics, you may challenge him to rebel, become intrigued, and want to learn even more – often without your knowledge or guidance.

PARENTS:

Instead of forbidding materials that are violent, explain why you are concerned. Go through the materials together, so that you can teach your son how to handle it appropriately. Ask questions, engage him in discussions, and teach him what is appropriate and what is not. Just remember, saying "no" will not work forever and will often encourage him to seek out materials behind your back.

TEACHERS:

When a boy wants to read something that may be too violent, don't instantly say no. Examine the material, and if needed, let his parents know. Use the expertise of a librarian if needed.

TIP #

46

TEACH HIM HOW TO FIND READING MATERIALS

Struggling boy readers are often too shy or embarrassed to ask for help. If he is reluctant to find reading materials, find out why. Maybe he's overwhelmed, confused, frustrated, or has some other issue.

The more he senses that you want to help him, the more likely he will want to put forth the effort to learn.

Convince him that reading = learning = independence.

Take him by the hand, literally if needed, and walk around the library, bookstore, classroom, grocery store, or even online. Read my article:

http://www.GettingBoysToRead.com/12Tips

47 DO MORE THAN ALLOW MOVEMENT; REQUIRE IT

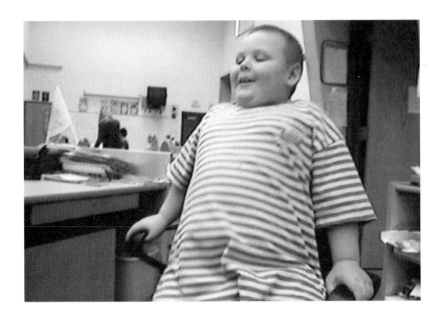

Far too often, boys are looked down upon and even scolded for being fidgety. Adults should be more than tolerant to his natural need for movement - both teachers and parents should deliberately schedule time throughout the day to allow his body to get the movement that his brain demands. How can we expect boys to become readers if we fail to allow his body the movement it needs and prepare his brain for periods of stillness?

PARENTS:

It will be a lot easier to entice your son to read AFTER he has some movement. Have him ride his bike, jump on a tramp, or shoot some hoops. A few minutes will usually do the trick. Ask his teacher if he is getting enough "brain breaks" or other opportunities for movement during the school day.

TEACHERS:

Never take away his recess! If you must punish him for something, find another way. If bad weather cancels outdoor recess, make sure your boys have some type of movement indoors. Many highly respected teachers (at all levels) make sure that their students have various forms of movement throughout the day. Brain breaks are vital.

TIP #

48 Connect Him With The Pros: Librarians!

Teacher-Librarian Joyce Valenza - www.Twitter.com/JoyceValenza

As librarians, we are trained experts who are freely available to both you and your boys for help. We know thousands of great books, magazines, and websites. We work with many different struggling boy readers, and most of us are naturally empathetic and eager to help - so reach out to us with details of your needs and concerns. The more librarians you ask for help, the better; all readers benefit from multiple perspectives.

TIP

49 NEVER CRITICIZE WHAT HE LIKES TO READ

I t doesn't matter if his book seems too easy, too hard, against your tastes, strange, boring, silly, or immature. If you make him feel badly he will resent you and eventually disengage as a reader.

TIP # 50

AVOID OVERUSING 'GIRL' THEMES

Boys look for books they can relate to. If they sense the book is meant for girls, most of the time they will disengage, especially as they get older. This includes girls on the front cover, in the content, photos, illustrations, and especially as the main character. It doesn't matter if the book is fiction, nonfiction, a picture book, sports, vehicles, comics, graphic novels, or anything else – boys will relate more to books that focus on other boys.

One of my favorite fiction books is, *The True Confessions of Charlotte Doyle*, by Avi. It's a murder mystery that is filled with action, suspense, and even pirates! Despite my best efforts, I've always struggled getting boys to read it because once they discover it's a book about a 13-year old girl, most boys say no.

Similarly, don't mock him if he likes "girlie" books. Some boys love *Twilight*, and shouldn't be made to feel less masculine.

TIP
51

JUDGE A BOOK BY ITS COVER...

Boys do and so should you. Boys are visual by nature and what they see FIRST makes an impression. Visuals influence their attitudes and decisions about reading the book.

Book publishers invest TONS of time and money to create the best book covers possible. As adults, we also formulate our first impressions visually; so, when you are trying to find a book he may like, pretend you are him when looking at the cover.

TIP

52

SURPRISE HIM WITH RESEARCH

Do the legwork for him every once in a while by spending a few minutes researching and printing a few on-line articles or blog posts on a topic he is curious about. If possible, take it one step further and check out a few similar books from the library. Call attention to your kind gesture by saying something like this: "I know you're interested in skateboards, so I decided to do something nice for you. I spent some time looking up information about skateboards; I also took it one step further and found some things at the library. I don't want to pressure you - I just want you to know that I was thinking about you. Here you go…"

53

Let Him Know That It's Okay To Leave A Nonfiction Book Unfinished

Most boys have a false sense of failure when they do not finish an entire book. It's been drilled into their brains since day one - start from the beginning and read everything, all the way to the very end. The truth, however, is that

most nonfiction readers only read the parts they need.

Once they get what they want, they disregard the rest of the book and move on. Boys who love nonfiction and don't know this may experience a sense of guilt and failure. As a result, they risk damaging their reader self-esteem. It's up to you to teach him that only reading "excerpts" is common and acceptable when he reads.

TIP

54

TEACH HIM HOW TO FIND LIBRARY BOOKS

Teacher-Librarian Christy Yacano

The key here is to acknowledge his need for independence. Help him learn to find a book by:

1. physically browsing through the shelves
2. using the computer to search the library collection, and
3. asking a librarian for keyword ideas (especially if he's shy)

These techniques can help him uncover specific titles to match his needs, by himself. This is very important, especially as he gets older.

Know The 10 Reasons Why Boys Don't Like To Read:

1. Lack of male role models
2. Lack of educated parents and teachers
3. Low self-confidence as a reader
4. Poor reading environment
5. Negative experiences
6. Stereotype that reading makes him look weak
7. Other priorities/distractions (TV, games, activities)
8. Lack of exposure to interesting materials
9. Disconnection with required reading
10. He actually likes to read, but needs help redefining what "counts" as reading

TIP # 56
CONNECT READING WITH HIS CULTURE

Connecting reading with his ethnic background can be an inspiring, effective way to build your relationship and strengthen his sense of pride and self-worth.

Step 1 - Start with a Conversation:

Meet with him in private and have a brief, heart-to-heart talk about his ethnic background. Ask him to share some of his background knowledge, opinions, and feelings about his culture. Explain that you value his culture and want to learn more. Tell him that there are hundreds of biographies online about famous people of all ethnic backgrounds - athletes, musicians, politicians, peace activists, artists, and many more.

Step 2 - Research Successful Guys:

Use the info from your conversation and do a quick Google search to find three or four biographical articles about guys (either boys or men) from his ethnic background who:

- overcame hardships
- became successful
- would be positive influences

Make sure the articles include photos, and try to find successful guys who relate to his hobbies or interests. Offer to research together, but, if needed, do the research yourself.

Step 3 - Inspire Him to Learn More:

Sit down with him again later on, in private, for a brief follow-up conversation. Before you handover the printouts, give him a brief teaser about something you read so that he is inspired to read the article. Read it aloud with him and discuss things along the way.

Interview with Jane Yolen, Author of Owl Moon

Jane Yolen - www.JaneYolen.com

Below, Ms. Yolen discusses how to help struggling readers.

MIKE MCQUEEN:

How do we help struggling readers?

JANE YOLEN:

I think that we have to acknowledge that some people are natural readers. My oldest two were natural readers. Heidi was reading at four; Adam was reading at two-and-a-half. And, in fact, the nursery school teacher would say, "Now kids, when you finish your projects, go over to the corner and Adam will read to you." He was two-and-a-half and three at the time.

The youngest one, Jason, did not start reading till he was seven, and we were all pretty frustrated at that point because he clearly loved books; he loved having stories read to him. But, when he tried to read the stories, they didn't sound like the stories we were reading to him.

But, one day, I went in to tuck him in bed, and I saw him reading, and what he was reading was not *Hop on Pop*, which I was trying to teach him to read, or *Green Eggs and Ham*; he just kept on looking at me and saying "but... but... it's the same thing over and over; I don't know where I am."

He was sitting in bed and he was reading – sounding out and reading *Peterson's Bird Guide*, both the English and the Latin, because that was what his interest was. He went birding with his father, who was a huge birder, and to this day he reads nonfiction. He's not a fiction reader.

And sometimes we miss the fact that kids may be reading something. Maybe they're reading comic books, maybe they're reading graphic novels, maybe they're reading cereal boxes, maybe they're reading the sports page, and we have to go where they are, not where we want them to be. And I think that's the difference. I think that teachers and parents, because I was one of them, get very frustrated if the child isn't reading "up to standard", the books you want him to read. And it may not be the books he wants to read. A really good teacher, a really good librarian will help them find the books that will turn them on. But they may not be the books that we approve of.

To listen to our entire interview, visit:

www.GettingBoysToRead.com/JaneYolen

CHAPTER 4:

LURE HIM WITH THE BEST MATERIALS

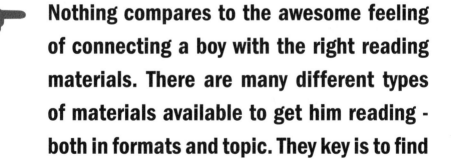

Nothing compares to the awesome feeling of connecting a boy with the right reading materials. There are many different types of materials available to get him reading - both in formats and topic. They key is to find materials that he can't resist.

57 EXPAND THE DEFINITION OF READING

The world of reading is not limited to what appears in printed books. Information is delivered using a variety of vehicles, including, but not limited to: magazines, audiobooks, comics, newspapers, eBooks, web sites, Tweets, and Facebook posts.

Far too often, boys lose self-esteem as readers early on in their academic career, because adults incorrectly limit the definition of reading to required school assignments. If boys don't hear the expanded definition of reading, many may begin developing a negative attitude, which worsens as they age.

Boys who respect themselves as readers have more reading confidence, read more often, and are willing to take more reading risks. As adults, we must understand, agree, and teach this broader definition to our boys. Above all, we must never make him feel bad for what types of materials and formats he likes to read, especially as he grows and his interests change.

TIP #

58   HELP HIM DEFINE HIS FAVORITE READING MATERIALS

The following is a list of reading materials many boys enjoy reading. Go through this list with him and give him examples so he understands each type of reading. Have him rate each item on a scale of 1 to 10. After that, discuss his favorite three or four choices. Ask him questions about why he likes those materials and most importantly

remind him that all of these materials count as reading!

Types of Reading:

- Nonfiction
- Magazines
- Picture books
- Fiction
- Comic books or graphic novels
- E-Reading: eBooks, texts, social media

- Online articles
- Jokes
- How-to articles/books
- Biographies
- Newspaper
- Strange and trivial facts
- Trading cards
- Manuals (Repair something, build a Lego, etc.)

TIP #

59

KNOW THE DIFFERENCE BETWEEN COMICS AND GRAPHIC NOVELS

Many parents and teachers don't know very much about comic books or graphic novels, not to mention differences between the two. Knowing these differences can help you introduce and guide him to whichever best suits his needs.

Comic Books:

Features that separate them from graphic novels include:

- **Content**: Superheroes are the most popular subject in comic books, followed by character-based themes like Garfield, The Simpsons, etc.
- **Physical Properties**: Comic books are often made of super thin, magazine-like paper.
- **Length**: They are very short, often 32 pages or fewer.
- **Audience**: Preteens through adults.
- **Collectible**: Comic books are highly collectible.

Graphic Novels:

Features that separate them from comic books include:

- **Content**: Graphic novels cover almost every topic you can imagine. Fictional stories are the most established type, but nonfiction graphic novels are increasing in popularity.
- **Physical Properties**: They often resemble the length, width, and thickness of typical fiction novels.
- **Length**: Varies greatly. Some are made for new readers and can consist of as few as eight pages; others, for advanced readers, can be up to 300 pages. Generally speaking, graphic novels are longer than comic books.
- **Audience**: Preschool through adults of all ages.
- **More Accepted** – Graphic novels are much more popular in schools than comic books.

60 LET HIM READ COMIC BOOKS

Boys love comic books because they are small, bite-sized chunks of entertaining information. Comic books appeal to boys' visual nature, love for superheroes, and passion to collect things.

Over the years I've had many talks with different men about reading. I'm surprised at how often comic books come into our conversation. They love to reminisce on their childhood memories of comic books – both reading and collecting them.

Unfortunately, most teachers and parents frown upon a boy's obsession with comic books. They can often worry that comic books aren't academically challenging enough. The truth is comic books can have significant literary merit.

When a boy picks up on this negative attitude, either directly or indirectly, he may internalize the message his reading preferences are substandard or even wrong. Set him on the right track and praise him for being a reader.

TIP # 61

GUIDE HIM TO COMIC BOOK APPS

There are dozens of free or inexpensive apps available for him to read and engage with on mobile devices. Many apps offer a free preview, which is a great way to peak his interest and let him test-drive the comic book. I love the extremely vibrant high-resolution color display when reading on mobile devices. And yes, so do boys.

TIP # 62 Buy Him A Magazine At The Grocery Store (Parents)

Once per month, bring your son grocery shopping and start your visit at the magazine display. If needed, point out a few issues he may like and give him unpressured time to browse through them.

Tell him you will buy one, but he needs to take his time and look through them. If he's old enough, go about your shopping and have him catch up with you when he's done. If he requires your supervision, take a moment and look for one yourself. This will take the pressure off him to hurry up and it will also allow you to

model what adult readers do.

63

Buy Him A Subscription To Boys' Life Magazine

Boys' Life magazine has been inspiring boys to read for over 100 years. Their magazine and website are both packed with:

- Great content that boys love, such as humor, adventure, and hands-on activities
- Short articles that are quick to read and lots of fun
- Tons of great photos and graphics
- Visually appealing information with great text features

64 ASK A LIBRARIAN FOR EXTRA MAGAZINES

Teacher-Librarian Dean Raizman

Each month, libraries discard dozens of outdated magazines that are in great shape and would be perfect for most boys. Pop into your nearby library and explain you have a boy (or boys) who is struggling and would love the old issues. If you can't get them at that moment, ask the librarian to set aside a small pile and suggest you can return later. Remember - the squeaky wheel gets the grease.

TIP

65 LEARN ABOUT E-READING

When used properly, technology can help motivate boys and improve their reading skills. More electronic reading occurs with boys than most adults realize. Online articles, social media, mobile devices, and even video games are packed with a variety of literary opportunities.

An e-Reader is **ANY** electronic device that enables you to read on it. Examples include iPads, Kindles, Nooks, computers, smart phones - even music and gaming devices. The technological advances of portable devices have EXPLODED over the past few years. There are now hundreds of millions of devices sold each year that can support e-Reading. As long as he avoids becoming a Screen Zombie (see previous Tip), eReading can be a great spark to keep him reading. If you need help learning,

Let him teach you!

Have him demonstrate his prowess as a 21st-century learner. If he's not familiar with eReading, explain to him you could use a little bit of help in figuring it out. Get him access to an eReading device and then ask him if he'd be willing to try to figure out how to use it, and then teach you. If you are both already familiar with eReaders, challenge each other by asking technical questions about reading eBooks on the device. The idea is to give him a chance to be "the expert" and in the process spark his interest in eReading.

TIP

66 ENGAGE HIM IN DIGITAL STORYTELLING

Digital storytelling is the practice of using multimedia-based tools to tell a true or fictional story. These stories often include a combination of video, audio, text, animations, and graphics. Boys can be both producers and consumers of digital storytelling, which makes for a great 21st century literacy experience.

Most boys love the electronic nature of digital storytelling because:

- It's interactive

- He can often control his literacy experience
- It's hands-on
- It's visually and auditorily stimulating
- He has ownership in the creation process

There are many great digital storytelling tools that are either free or very inexpensive. Here are just a few:

- Animoto
- Powtoon
- Voice Thread
- Story Bird
- Capzles
- Domo Animate
- Make Beliefs Comix
- iMovie
- Windows Movie Maker
- Pic-Lits
- Pixton
- ZooBurst

67 Use Amazon's "Related Titles"

Customers Who Bought This Item Also Bought

The I'M NOT SCARED Book
> Todd Parr
★★★★★ (11)
Hardcover
$8.99

It's Okay To Be Different
> Todd Parr
★★★★★ (75)
Paperback
$6.29

This trick is so easy, yet it's often overlooked. Visit Amazon.com and find a book he has previously liked. Scroll to the bottom and browse the "Related Titles" area. When he sees a title he likes, click on it, read through the description, and then repeat the process.

TIP # 68   HELP HIM FIND BLOGS

RALPHFLETCHER.COM

BOOKS   WRITER'S THOUGHTS   TIPS FOR YOUNG WRITERS   TEACHER HANGOUT   Q&A WITH RALPH   EVENTS   BIO   CONTACT

Q&A with Ralph

Home / Q&A with Ralph

This shows me doing a school author visit. Happy guy!   These kids are reading Fig Pudding!   Me with my grandson, Solomon.

Blogs are content-rich treasure-troves that provide information on every topic imaginable. There are many different types of blogs, but most have these things in common:

- A shared interest between the author and audience
- a way for the audience to contribute their thoughts and opinions
- on-going news and information relating to the topic

Older boys love blogs because they can instantly be connected to their current interests. Help him find the blog that fits his needs by simply opening Google and entering "blogs about XYZ" (insert his hobby or interest). There are many blogs for adults, so filter as needed. Ask a librarian if you need help.

TRY eBOOKS

Here are 7 reasons why eBooks are great!

1) Interactivity

Thanks to digital technology, eBooks provide many opportunities for engagement such as: writing notes, searching for content, clicking links, listening to audio, watching videos, looking up definitions, and sometimes playing games that relate to the book. The ability to interact entices him to read and expand his learning.

2) "Brain Ready" Reading

Since a boy's brain needs his body to move frequently, carrying an eBook in his pocket or backpack allows more opportunities for "brain ready" reading. Each time he stands up, walks around, or sits down his brain gets recharged and is ready to read.

3) Accessibility

The ability to carry around an endless supply of reading materials opens up more reading opportunities compared to lugging around big, heavy books everywhere. There are many "off times" throughout each day such as sitting in the car or waiting around for something or someone. Get him to take advantage of these times with eBooks.

4) Chunk-able Text

As a struggling boy reader, small fonts were intimidating and frustrating to me. I hated the hopeless feeling that it would take forever until I was able to turn the page and feel like I was making progress in the book. With eBooks, the pages are smaller and the font size can be adjusted to suit his needs. Shorter pages give him a SENSE OF PROGRESS and ACCOMPLISHMENT, which builds his confidence at each "swipe" of the page. This empowerment is especially important when he faces challenging text.

5) Visually Appealing

Since most boys prefer a lot of visually stimulating information, the vibrant color and crisp text projected from high-definition devices is more eye-catching than the dull, static display of ink on paper. Non-fiction books loaded with lots of zoom-able color photographs are dreams come true for many boys.

6) The Cool Factor

eBook devices provide the "Cool" factor that can draw boys into reading, in a way that print materials may not. Boys often love to impress others with cool things, especially electronic gadgets.

7) Incognito

As boys get older, many become self-conscious about being seen with printed books; they become afraid of looking like a "book nerd" among their peers (a sad, but true, reality). eBooks can help them be discrete when reading from a mobile device

Check out the eBooks I've created by visiting www.MikeMcQueen.com/Books

70 GUIDE HIM TO TEXT THAT IS SHORT & VISUALLY APPEALING

Many boys prefer shorter, bite-sized pieces of text that contain photos, charts, and other graphical information. Sometimes this preference is because of reading problems, while other times it's simply a lack of patience.

If you work with boys who are really struggling or resistant, use other techniques mentioned in this book and also be sure to connect them with reading materials that they can

get through quickly and feel successful.

Examples of short, visual texts include: magazines, online articles, How-to nonfiction, picture books, comics, etc...

TIP
71 REMIND HIM THAT HE "IS A READER!"

As boys get older, many will come to a false belief that they don't like to read. The truth is, they will love reading **IF** they can find materials that meet their interests and needs.

I always tell boys,

"You like to read; you just need some help connecting to the right materials."

After a few strategic questions and 10 minutes of careful looking, most agree with me.

72 INSPIRE HIM WITH HOW-TO MATERIALS

Author and illustrator Spencer Nelson

Boys love to read for a purpose! How-to books give us a reason to read and reinforce the notion that reading helps us to accomplish something.

How-to reading materials often connect us with things that we like to do with our hands. Many men read fix-it manuals and books or magazines that teach us how to build things.

Common How-to Topics:

- Create, build, or fix things (models, cars, paper airplanes, inventions, home repair, Legos, forts, etc.)
- Improve techniques in a sport or hobby
- Make money
- Become a... (career)
- Solve problems or play games
- Draw or shape things
- Do cool science experiments
- Learn new skills
- Teach pets obedience or tricks
- Get in shape
- Operate remote-control vehicles
- Tell jokes
- Collect bugs
- Gross out friends
- Defend yourself
- Survive
- Start or maintain collections
- Play games or do tricks
- Use gadgets, tools, or devices

In the photo above, I'm standing with Spencer Nelson, author and illustrator of How to Draw Monsters and Aliens. If you know a boy who is artistic and/or loves monsters, get this book for him; it is the best How-to-Draw book I've ever seen. It's filled with awesome illustrations, the content is very organized, and it does a great job teaching kids how to draw.

Interview with David Warlick, Author of Redefining Literacy 2.0

David Warlick - www.OnLearning.us

Below, Mr. Warlick discusses the advances in defining literacy and reading.

MIKE MCQUEEN:

In your book, you mention the idea of, "exposing what is true." What does this mean in relation to struggling boy readers?

DAVID WARLICK:

When I was growing up, everything I read came through filters: the librarian, publishers, editors - everything came through a filter, so what we had access to read was approved of by someone. When one-sided information is printed, readers' literary exposure becomes incredibly limited or filtered.

Today, readers have access to the whole library, the whole global library. It's a new fresh environment that almost anyone can publish to, almost anything they want, for almost any reason they want -- and this is a good thing. We have an opportunity to expand our knowledge over the next few years, in an unprecedented way because of this open, real-time communication. The internet at our fingertips changes or expands what it means to be literate, what it means to be a reader today. It's as important to determine what's true, what's accurate, what's relevant, what's appropriate, and what's valid, in terms of being able to analyze where the information is coming from, how you found it, and its accessibility as a text.

When I was growing up all, all I needed to know was how to use an index, a table of contents, and have a basic mastery of the alphabet. Today, you Google it. You start with billions of pages of information and, quite frankly, if you are not able to use something like Google, I might just assume you've been struck with information overload. Although siphoning through information on the internet is not necessarily the kind of reading we aim towards as adults, and measure or encourage in the classroom, today's generation of learners are likely reading and writing more than any other generation.

MIKE MCQUEEN:

Right! And that's part of the issue with boys thinking; they don't like to read books, or parents or teachers worry their boys don't like to read, but in a sense they are probably pretty engaged readers. Certainly after you take into account the redefined version of literacy.

DAVID WARLICK:

Yes, and it's a different kind of reading. It's more of a working reading; they're reading because they want to find out how to get to the next level of the video game; they're reading because they want to learn how to put this effect into a video or whatever. Working reading or this reading style when working, is quite possibly asking students to read more, in terms of reading in the classroom.

MIKE MCQUEEN:

What common obstacles or fears do parents and teachers have about redefining literacy? I'm sure you've talked with lots of people; what fears or things get in the way of thinking that reading is more than just looking at a book or a newspaper?

DAVID WARLICK:

I think the biggest obstacle is momentum. There is this prevailing sense that literacy is about the three Rs: the ability to read, the ability to do arithmetic, and of course, writing. It's a model we have grown up with; it's a model we have spent 12 or 13 years in school learning. I consider any skill requiring information processing to accomplish a goals or goals to be a literacy skill.

To listen to our entire interview, visit:
http://www.GettingBoysToRead.com/DavidWarlick

CHAPTER 5:

MAKE READING INTERACTIVE

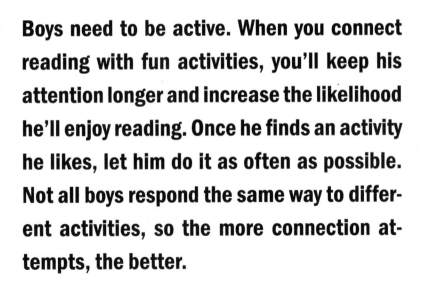

Boys need to be active. When you connect reading with fun activities, you'll keep his attention longer and increase the likelihood he'll enjoy reading. Once he finds an activity he likes, let him do it as often as possible. Not all boys respond the same way to different activities, so the more connection attempts, the better.

MAKE A MESSY PILE

I've see hundreds of reluctant readers fall in love with books simply by getting their hands on them. Collect a pile of different reading materials he may be interested in and scatter them on a table in a mixed up mess. "Accidentally" spill them on the floor if needed. With a sad face, explain that you could really use his help – both his muscles and opinions. Tell him you are looking for reading materials other guys might like, and you'd appreciate his opinion. Ask him to BRIEFLY skim through the pile and sort them into "Like It" or "Leave It." Afterwards, if he still looks willing to help, ask him to help put them back on the shelves.

TIP
74

TEACH HIM TO
WRITE IN THE TEXT

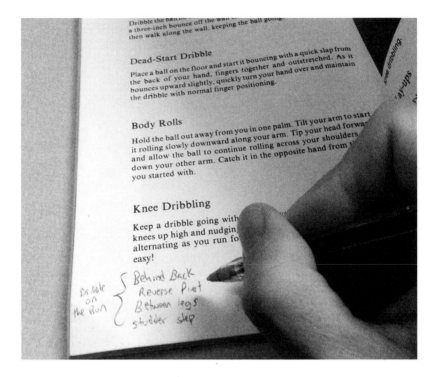

ince many boys are visual/spatial learners, a great way to process and organize their thoughts, keep them engaged, and improve comprehension is to teach them to write or draw in the text. If writing in the book or magazine is not an option, have them use sticky notes or a separate journal. To get their buy-in, teach them why this technique is important. Model the process and encourage them to be fun and creative with the writing techniques they use. Remember that doodling is great!

TIP # 75

MAKE INSTANT MINI-BOOKS

Boys love to do things with their hands. They love to take things apart, examine the pieces, and put them back together. Take advantage of his innate desire to build things and teach him how to make an instant mini book.

It's quick, easy, and – best of all – free! All you need is a cell phone camera, printer, scissors, glue, and crayons or markers. To learn how and see examples, visit:

www.GettingBoysToRead.com/InstantMiniBooks

TIP

76 | TAKE RESEARCH-BASED FIELD TRIPS

The idea is simple – plan a fun place to visit and prepare ahead of time by doing research.

Here are a few examples:

- Find an upcoming car show, but before going, look up some information about his favorite vehicle.
- Have him study a bug or animal that he loves, then take him to the zoo to learn more.
- Before going on a family trip or vacation, do some background reading about the destination.

TIP
77
TAKE HIM TO THE LIBRARY - OFTEN

Teacher-Librarian Angie Wagner

Take advantage of both your school library and your neighborhood public library, especially if you are fortunate enough to have one close by. Libraries have tens of thousands of great books and magazines, as well as many free and fun events. I always recommend that students visit the library at least once per week. Eventually, with enough library visits, he will feel comfortable and willing to take risks with finding books and asking for help. You have a chance to inspire his love for the library, to plant a seed that will stay with him throughout his entire life, but it's up to you to make sure he gets there.

78 | ASK LIBRARIANS FOR HELP

Teacher-Librarian Sophie Blavet

Both school and public librarians are hidden gems who can be a vital resource for parents and teachers. When teachers or parents confide in us about students who needs help, we'll go out of our way to get him or her the help needed. We'll get to know him, help him find information or reading materials, and even team with other staff to address his needs. Most of us have master's degrees, huge hearts and the desire to help, but it's UP TO YOU TO ASK.

TIP
79

HAVE HIM DOODLE DURING READ ALOUD

Drawing by Author and Illustrator Mark Ludy - www.MarkLudy.com

When a boy is listening to a story, you can help him avoid auditory overload by giving him a tactile activity. Drawing or doodling helps him concentrate and keeps his mind focused and engaged in the text, especially if you use the read aloud techniques mentioned in this book.

Thanks to author, Mark Ludy, for this great image. Visit his web site at www.MarkLudy.com

80 BUY HIM A GIFT CARD TO A BOOKSTORE

It's extremely easy to buy a gift card online or at a nearby grocery store. Reach into your purse or wallet, buy the gift card, and then take him to the bookstore and let him pick whatever reading material he wants. Make your only requirement that the item has some type of reading in it. That means magazines, comic books, or whimsical paper airplane books are okay!

TIP # 81

HAVE HIM ORGANIZE THE CLASSROOM LIBRARY (TEACHERS)

Dedicate a section of the room to be the Classroom Library. Ask him to go through whatever books are available and organize them however he sees fit. Give him labels, baskets, special shelves, and anything else to help him make the space fun and inviting. If needed, ask him to choose a friend to help, preferably one who knows books.

82   Take A Tour Of The Library

Since most boys are visual/spatial learners, taking a walking tour around the library is very important. Don't accept that he already knows where things are and how to find materials – hardly any boys truly know. Walk around with him and point things out, especially where magazines and nonfiction books are and how everything is organized. Be sure to explain tips for "browsing" and how to find specific topics and titles that he might need. Ask a librarian to guide you, but if he's against the idea you should lead the way.

TIP # 83

DO A READING WALKABOUT (TEACHERS)

Accommodate his brain's need for movement by organizing a "Reading Walkabout." Plan a short walking loop (inside or outside) that is close, easy to monitor, and not too difficult to maneuver. The concept is that he and a partner will walk this loop while engaging in a discussion about a short, interesting text. Print out a few guiding questions and explain the purpose and process for the walkabout.

Pair him with a well-behaved, trustworthy partner and require that they take turns asking questions and always are engaged in conversation. Make sure they know the route and behavior expectations. If you are worried about accounting for their whereabouts, position yourself in the hallway, create a shorter loop, and have them check in with you as they pass. After 10-15 minutes, return to the starting point and debrief as a class. Reward his success with lots of praise.

84 SET UP A BOOK CLUB FOR BOYS

One of the best ways to impact a large group of boys is to organize a "boys only" book club. If done correctly, it can be short, simple, fun, and very effective. Read my blog post to see how we launched one and how it IMMENSELY impacted our at-risk school: www.GettingBoysToRead.com/GuysRead

85 MODIFY READING INCENTIVE PROGRAMS (TEACHERS)

I've seen many boys "come alive" as readers with computer-based reading incentive programs. I've developed a love-hate relationship over the years because there are both pros and cons to them.

These programs appeal to many boys because:

- when he reads to earn prizes, it taps into his natural urge to COMPETE
- it gives him a good REASON TO READ
- the incentives can be MEANINGFUL and FUN (at least in the short term)

Aside from the huge expense, the main problem with these programs is they tailor almost exclusively to fiction readers and do not support the natural reading preferences of most boys – magazines, on-line information, comics, and especially nonfiction books.

Here are a few ways to modify a program to accommodate the diverse needs of many boy readers:

- Double or triple the points for nonfiction tests.
- Allow other ways to earn points: magazines, online articles, and other materials that don't have premade quizzes.
- Make the program a small part of their grade. It should only be a supplement to the skills they are learning with reading.

86   VISIT A COMIC BOOK STORE

When I popped into a small, local comic book store to look around, I was AMAZED at the quantity and variety of comic books and collectible figurines. There was a fun vibe that filled the room with excitement, enticing me to look around and join this huge society of fans. Little stores like this one can be found all over the city. Do a quick Google search, find one, and take him on a field trip. It will be inexpensive, memorable, and loads of fun.

87 ATTEND A COMIC BOOK EVENT

T hroughout the country there are humongous comic book con-
ventions called ComicCon, attracting millions of comic book
fanatics each year. These events are invigorating for both new
and veteran comic book enthusiasts of all ages. I attend ComicCon
in Denver each year and am blown away by the different authors,
artists, collectors, and thousands of comic book fans. It's a fun experience for everyone and is an extremely inspiring way to get him
fired up to read.

TIP # 88

Host a "Read and Feed"

Over the years, our library has hosted dozens of our famous and extremely popular, "Free Pancake Days". For each 2-hour event, we cook about 2,000 pancakes and invite students and staff from our entire school to take a little break and have some relaxed fun in the library.

We display books, play music, eat pancakes, and just hang out in the ultimate reading atmosphere. Read and Feed events build a fun connection for boys.

PARENTS:

Take your son and his buddies to the library or bookstore, followed by a pizza party and book or magazine discussion.

TEACHERS:

You can host a simplified "Read and Feed" in your classroom by inviting kids to bring snacks from home as well as a pillow or other comfort object.

HAVE HIM PARTNER READ

Partner Reading can be a fun and extremely powerful tool to get boys reading, especially if you connect him with another guy and teach them both how to do it properly. Have them both watch my instructional video and then check that they actually follow my advice: www.GettingBoysToRead.com/PartnerReading

The "Partner Reading Checklist":

- pick something to fun to read
- sit side-by-side
- take turns
- discuss what you read

PARENTS:

Recruit friends, relatives, and neighbors to partner/read with your son. After they read, have them do an activity related to what they read. For example: partner read a skateboard magazine and then have them visit a skate park.

TEACHERS:

Set up a weekly "Study Buddies" program and then get both classes excited by giving a "pep talk" about Partner Reading. Have the class rotate partners. Set up a "Partner Reading" event at your library, school, or local bookstore. Check out this page from Reading Rockets: www.ReadingRockets.Org/Strategies/Partner_Reading

TIP

90

READ MY INTERACTIVE eBooks With Him

Interactive eBooks are a cool, innovative way for boys to read. Take advantage of these books by using them to bond and strengthen your reading relationship with him. Ask questions and discuss different features that make these books interactive - audio, video, photo galleries, 3-D, quizzes, notes, animations, etc.

One of my life-long goals as an author is to create dozens, if not hundreds, of interactive eBooks for kids. Check out my books and stay connected with me as I develop more and more each year - www.MikeMcQueen.com/Books

Interview with Cris Tovani, Author of I Read It, but I Don't Get It: Comprehension Strategies for Adolescent Readers

Cris Tovani - <www.TovaniGroup.com>

Below, Ms. Tovani discusses how to help struggling readers with comprehension.

MIKE MCQUEEN:

What are some things that we can do to help boys with comprehension?

CRIS TOVANI:

A lot of struggling readers who I have worked with over the

past 15 years have had tons and tons of phonics instructions and fluency work. Because they have endured a lot of phonics instruction, many of them feel they're just not good readers. They've been in reading classes since the first grade, they're still in reading classes, so they just can't do it. We are giving them more of what they don't need.

Of course, there are kids out there who need systematic reading instruction, especially new language speakers and beginning readers. However, by the time they get into high school, most struggling readers have been taught decoding strategies, but have not been taught ways to produce meanings of unfamiliar words.

When students only get phonics instruction they don't know how to help themselves when meaning breaks down. They don't know how to go back and change the way they've read -- in essence, how to teach themselves the right way to read. They don't know how to re-read selectively with the purpose in mind. My favorite class to teach is probably a class of struggling readers because they get just a little twinkle in their eyes when they realize they're not dumb, that they can make a sense of text when they are given a few helpful strategies to access the text differently; it still tickles me. It's so gratifying to see that, to help them build that efficacy so that they can be better readers, that it's not too late for them.

My first two books taught how to help kids read without being a reading specialist and how to be a better reader of your subject matter. Good instruction circles back to modeling - whatever you do as an expert reader should provide teachers with strategies to say to kids, "Okay, here's what you can do when you don't get it. Go back and try this."

Athletic coaches practice this method often. They'll circle

back and model for kids: "Try it again, try it this way, and see what happens."

MIKE MCQUEEN:

Let's talk about parallel experiences; I know you mentioned that a little bit. Tell us, what are parallel experiences and what can we do with them?

CRIS TOVANI:

I started to discover this when I began teaching kids in high school; teachers in my building would ask me to come into their science class, or especially math classes, and try helping kids to be better readers. I realized I was a much better reading teacher when I was reading outside of my comfort zone. Unfamiliar with content, I was forced to apply reading strategies to make sense of the text, like a parallel experience. A lot of times, teachers become experts in their content area because they are reading the same subject matter all of the time. As a result, they aren't necessarily equipped to help struggling readers because they have not been forced to move outside of their comfort zone to develop strategies that support struggling readers.

Read outside of your comfort zone and notice what you do when you come across something uninteresting to you. How do you construct meaning? Do you have to annotate the text when you read something you do not possess any background knowledge? How do you build that background knowledge?

Now think about how this applies to your kids who don't have background knowledge. You have strategies, but that student might not. What do you do to help that student? What I discovered about myself is that I tend to ask questions. If I have to read something brand new, I'm annotating questions all the way down the margins. Then, I go to somebody or someplace where I could build that background knowledge. A lot of times, I go online and Google something; or, I might go to somebody who is an expert reader of that material and I'll ask him or her questions.

I figured out how to annotate when I had to read chemistry books. I went back into chemistry classes and modeled that process: read a little bit and then check to see what you remember. If you don't remember anything, give yourself a little job: try to paraphrase one sentence or try to ask a question.

Sometimes as teachers we get so good at reading our own subject matter we forget what it was like the first time we read. We forget what it was like to be a new reader. If we read outside of our comfort level and we watch what we do, when we encounter struggles that our kids have, we now have some strategies to go back and support them.

MIKE MCQUEEN:

It's kind of like empathy, then, to try to put yourself in their shoes to see what it's like.

CRIS TOVANI:

Absolutely; that's a great way to put it. For example, how can we remind ourselves and empathize with kids who are reading *The Great Gatsby* for the first time? When we read it at 16, we didn't get it either. After teaching it for 15 years, we forget where we were as teenagers and how frustrating it might have felt. How do we remember that? An English teacher might read a Russian novelist and see what that feels like, or a math teacher who is really good at geometry might pick up a calculus book and read outside of his comfort zone that way.

Too often, teachers trap themselves in their own thinking, "I'm not a reading specialist. I'm not an elementary school teacher." The truth is, you don't have to be either to teach kids how to read. Parents can help by watching their kids read. Is it clear to the parent their child is making sense of the information? How can they help their child make sense of unknown information? How can they model for their child what that looks like? Providing kids with these strategies is pretty empowering because when you show kids how to construct meaning, it means so much more than just decoding or fluency.

To listen to our entire interview, visit:
www.GettingBoysToRead.com/CrisTovani

INTERVIEW

Interview with Richard Selznick, Author of The Shutdown Learner: Helping Your Academically Discouraged Child

Dr. Richard Selznick - www.DrSelz.com

Below, Dr. Selznick discusses warning signs of the "shut-down" learner.

MIKE MCQUEEN:

What are the warning signs to look for with someone that is a shut-down learner?.

DR. SELZNICK:

The formula for the shut-down learner goes something like this: cracks in the foundation + time + a lack of understanding + strained patterns of family communication = a shut-down learner.

What are those cracks in the foundation? What are the first things that start to lead towards a person shutting down? As early as kindergarten, maybe even earlier, you can start to see signs of what will potentially later lead to a child being discovered as "shut-down."

These early signs are what you see when people talk about dyslexia and learning disabilities. They include things like letter naming, not just singing the alphabet song, but being able to name letters at four and five-years old, and understanding the sounds attached to the letters (phonemic awareness) – all of those activities.

When kids are "rolling around in circle time," they're not "misbehaving" because they're purely -- and often erroneously -- called kids with ADHD; they are inattentive because they have difficulty accessing those language functions necessary for circle time.

Children, typically around five-years old begin to show some of the potential shut-down learner indicators. Another indicator you might observe, is a child very positively loving things like Legos and other hands-on toys, and being a very visual child. Some people say, "Oh! So if my kid loves Legos, does that mean he is going to automatically become a shut-down learner?" No, but that combination of difficulty with phonemic awareness, rhyming and thriving with hands-on activities should be some of the indicators to monitor.

Instead of discounting behaviors typically observed beginning in the first grade -- those behaviors people far too often say, "Oh, you know how boys are, you should just wait it out." -- I take the very opposite approach and proactively look at reading development, spelling, basic decoding abilities, and how they are overall emerging as learners.

MIKE MCQUEEN:

So, it's like diving in right away.

DR. SELZNICK:

Correct, when referring back to the formula of cracks in the foundation + time, an important component of the child's struggles with learning begins in the early elementary school years. Perhaps to avoid panic, parents are mistakenly told to, "wait and see," if the behavior improves; however, cracks begin widening and time is passing, because of this lack of proactive understanding.

This lack of understanding leads us to the third component. Here we begin to think "he just doesn't like to read," "he's unmotivated," or "he just should try harder." To me, this demonstrates a lack of understanding because what's really contributing to the child showing those signs, are skill deficits he had back when those cracks were first ignored.

To listen to our entire interview, visit:
www.GettingBoysToRead.com/RichardSelznick

#6

MAKE READING FUN!

No matter what the topic, more learning occurs when the process is fun. John Medina, author of *Brain Rules*, says in chapter 4, "We don't pay attention to boring things." Based on my 20 years of experience as a teacher, librarian, and parent, one of the most important techniques in getting boys to read is to grab their attention by making it fun. When boys see reading as fun and meaningful, they will have a better attitude, learn more, and enjoy it more throughout their lives.

TIP

91

INTEGRATE HUMOR

Teacher & Author Patrick Allen - www.bit.ly/PatrickAllen

Boys love to smile and laugh. Always be on the lookout for ways to use humor, especially in relation to reading. Here are a few ideas:

- Act silly/goofy
- Make fun of your mistakes
- Find funny books
- Use gross humor
- Be physically animated
- Scare or startle him
- Tease him (with caution)
- Over-exaggerate
- Laugh out loud at funny things you read

TIP

92 MAKE READ ALOUD TIME A BLAST!

Reading aloud is the foundation to a lifelong love of reading. Follow these simple goals:

1. Read aloud **DAILY**
2. Make it **FUN**
3. Show **EMOTION**

Your positive energy and excitement becomes contagious and sends a message that reading is valuable and important. Vary the tone and volume of your voice. Be amazed about the things you read with him. Show how awesome it feels when reading solves a problem. Joke around every chance you can when you read together. In short, make reading a blast!

USE JOKE BOOKS

S pend a few bucks and buy a corny joke book filled with short, clean, and humorous jokes. Every once in a while pull out the book and lighten the mood.

KEEP HIM READING DURING SUMMER

SUMMER OUTDOOR READING CLUB

During summer break, many boys stop reading and lose the progress they made during the school year. Glen Todd, a superstar teacher with whom I have worked alongsidefor nine years, created a fun reading program with his kids called "The Summer Outdoor Reading Club." Listen to our audio interview to hear the awesome things he did to make reading a fun experience and keep kids on track:

www.GettingBoysToRead.com/SummerOutdoorReadingClub

TIP # 95

Don't Stress Him Out

Nothing sucks the fun out of a positive reading environment more than intense, in-your-face, worry-wart parents or teachers. Don't "hound" him about how little he reads, the type of material he likes, or how poor his skills are. Boys pick up on body language as well, so smile and encourage him often, despite the concerns or other issues you may be trying to suppress.

PARENTS:

No matter how worried you are about your son, don't connect his reading with your anger or frustrations. Don't pressure him or make him feel guilty. If you do, at some point he will shut down completely and his trust will be hard to regain.

TEACHERS:

Don't let the stress of standardized tests, fussy parents, or intense administrators rub off on him through you. Create a safe and relaxed environment within your classroom, even if it's a specific space within the room (once you're on the blue carpet with your book, you have a "bubble" where nothing else matters).

TIP
96

CREATE A READING PUPPET

Puppets can have an amazing reading impact on boys up to age nine or ten. This photo shows me with "Farmer Keet," my school's reading puppet. Farmer Keet's personality was a goofy character who loved books, but grew up without anyone ever sharing them with him. He came out of his pathetic house (box) once every few months for story time, followed by group discussion. After the story, students would ask him questions to see if he was listening. He then spent a few weeks floating around from classroom-to-classroom. Students loved to read to him and bring him to life, much like I modeled during story time.

If the puppet idea doesn't work, let him read to a pet and/or stuffed animal. Many struggling readers love reading to puppets or pets because it's fun and safe - they aren't judged on how good or bad they are reading.

TIP # 97

MODEL EXCITEMENT

Let him see and hear your passion for reading. It's not just WHAT you read, it's HOW you read it, and also what you say before and afterwards.

The more excited you get about reading, the more contagious it will be for him.

Change the volume and tone in your voice when you read aloud. Use nonverbal techniques -- overemphasize facial expressions, scream, shout, laugh, cry, and jump up and down! Do whatever it takes to show your emotions and make a positive, lasting impression about reading.

98 | LET HIM GET EXCITED

Boys can regularly be loud, and even obnoxious, when they get excited about things. As adults, we often stifle this excitement, fearing that boys will lose control and misbehave.

The two boys in the above photo literally ran in the library to the snakes section after I gave a nonfiction book talk to their class. When they found this book they screamed together, quite loudly, in excitement. If their teacher or I would have scolded them, their positive reading experience would have been tarnished or lost.

TIP

99

~~ALLOW~~ ENCOURAGE GROSS STUFF

S ome adults may cringe at boogers, farts, guts, and decaying things, but most boys naturally gravitate toward these gross topics. Be open-minded about boys reading gross materials, even if it goes against your preferences. Keep a handful of these types of books available at all times. Read my article, Boys and Gross Humor:

www.GettingBoysToRead.com/BoysAndGrossHumor

100

DON'T FORCE HIM

Forcing a boy to read something he dislikes is a bad idea. How you would feel about reading if someone required you to read on a topic that you found boring or unnecessary? You would feel angry and it's likely your attitude would plummet.

The more often you require him to read something he doesn't like, the more you risk turning him off to reading.

If you pressure him to read your books or articles and he doesn't like them, you could damage his confidence, attitude, and self-esteem as a reader. Follow the advice and tips in this book to lure or nudge him into reading – just don't force him.

TIP # 101

Play My Three Favorite Read Aloud Games

Most boys love games! We love the competition and appreciate having fun in the process. EVERY TIME I read aloud, I play one or more of the games below, which work with kids of all ages. I have become known throughout the community as a great storyteller, mostly because of these simple games:

1. **FILL IN THE BLANK:**

   At random times say the word, "blank" and ask him to fill it in. Simple, yet effective.

2. **PRANK WORDS:**

   As you read, every once in a while, substitute a word with something silly to see if he's listening. Act surprised when he catches you, and then keep reading.

3. **GOOD PART TEASER:**

   This is my favorite game. Pretend the next page is something amazing and that you "just can't show him, because it's so crazy cool it will freak him out!" It works on almost any page, in any book. Just be dramatic!

TIP
102

GET HIM A BOOK ON YO-YO TRICKS

As a culminating event to a Guys Read program, we took a group of 10-12-year old boys to Barnes and Noble to receive a free book. We were surprised when over half of them chose a yo-yo book. We respected their interests, bought the books, and returned to school. You should have seen the excitement as they huddled together in the library, their noses in the books, and their yo-yos in action. They loved teaching themselves tricks and showing off their skills as they improved.

The boys learned two important facts:

1. a bookstore has fun, cool books
2. reading can be a tool to teach them a skill

Interview with Steven Layne, Author of Igniting a Passion for Reading

Dr. Steven Layne - www.SteveLayne.com

Below, Dr. Layne discusses using magazines as tools for struggling readers.

MIKE MCQUEEN:

What are your thoughts are about magazines for struggling readers?

DR. LAYNE:

I often will say to parents, a really good way to help a disengaged child become engaged is to find a magazine related to a topic he or she will be interested in.

It's really, really crucial the subscription be taken out in the name of the child, so that your child receives mail with her or his name on it. Because we're adults, we often downplay the importance of small gestures – like receiving mail in your name. For kids, mail is a big deal, so having a magazine come on a regular basis is even better. When my older son's magazine arrives, he takes off on his own and reads that magazine cover to cover.

Comic books are another kind of magazine. I have kids, girls or boys, who really get into comic books; great, more power to them. A lot of vocabulary exists within comics. I was a big comic book collector as a kid. I learned a lot of great vocabulary from reading comic books.

MIKE MCQUEEN:

People underestimate the power hidden underneath the surface of comic books . . . There's a big festival every year – I'm sure they have it throughout the country – called StarFest. I went with a friend of mine; other attendees included all kinds of Star Wars fans and Star Trek fans. ComicFest was next door to StarFest – it was like a joint event. They had an enormous room packed with dozens and dozens of comic book vendors; I've never seen so many passionate comic book readers, I've never seen so many people passionate about reading like I did there. They talked for hours, and I've never seen so many different magazines; it's a world that I never knew existed. And you're right; there are hundreds and hundreds of different styles of comic books. Any other tips for struggling readers in particular that connects with magazines?

DR. LAYNE:

I think what you want to think about, when we think about magazines, is the fact that the layout is so different from a book. Parents, because they are not trained as educators, could certainly know the differences, but might not think about how the differences may positively impact their kids. It's also really common to see shorter stories in comics and magazines, so those are other advantages these choices bring to the table.

I try having reading materials in the car, bathroom, bedroom, etc. I try to teach my kids, when you have something to read, you're never bored and you will never have to be bored. So often kids are stuck in the car, so having reading materials accessible for them is a great way for them to pass the time.

MIKE MCQUEEN:

Right, easy access to visual support is huge, with all the photographs and illustrations. Moreover, there's academic merit in all sorts of nonfiction text features, headings, charts, graphs, and statistics.

To listen to our entire interview, visit:
www.GettingBoysToRead.com/StevenLayne

Interview with Kelly Gallagher, Author of Readicide: How Schools Are Killing Reading and What You Can Do About It

Kelly Gallagher - www.KellyGallagher.org

Below, Mr. Gallagher talks about high-interest materials.

MIKE MCQUEEN:

Why are high interest material important to struggling readers?

KELLY GALLAGHER:

I think high-interest reading materials are important to all readers, but particularly so for struggling readers. The problem is, because of testing demands, most of the reading kids are now being asked to do at school is academic in nature. I am a proponent of academic reading; I believe kids should read rich academic text. I want my ninth graders to read *Romeo and Juliet* or my twelfth graders to read *Hamlet*. But I also believe very, very strongly that kids should be encouraged to read recreationally, should be encouraged to read goofy and fun and not-so-serious reading; the kind of reading that Jon Scieszka calls "stupid reading."

That's the kind of reading that I think is really foundational to building a lifelong love of reading. Although it's foundational, I think it's being put on a back burner, or in many cases, it's actually being taken off the stove completely as the pressures mount on schools and teachers to raise the reading score, raise the reading score, raise the reading score. I like to read, but if I look at the reading activities that 'school' has asked my ninth graders to do over the years, I don't think that I would like reading very much either. These kids have come into my classroom, [after] No Child Left Behind was passed [2001] - they've now come to believe that is the reason why you should read: to prepare for a test.

I am getting ready to go on a summer vacation and I am excited because I have 10, 12, or 15 books that I have stacked and ready for my attention. Not one of them is academic in nature; it's not the kind of reading we do as life-long readers and yet schools have lost sight of that.

MIKE MCQUEEN:

Let's talk now about independent reading time - SSR (Sustained Silent Reading) or DEAR (Drop Everything and Read). Tell me what your thoughts are about those at school and at home.

KELLY GALLAGHER:

In this age of testing, SSR is sort of being shoved out. It's seen as not academic enough or, I don't know, not 'test preppy' enough. But, I strongly disagree with that attitude; if the kids are going to become readers they need three things: a book that's interesting, time to read it, and a place to read it. For some of my kids, the only place where all three of those practices intercept is at school.

Some of my kids have a place to read at home but they don't have time because they go to school and they go to soccer practice; they have to do the homework and they have to do this and that. Other kids, they have time to do it but they don't have the place to do it because they share the apartment with the brother or a large family.

So it seems to me that they only place where we can be assured that those three factors come together is at school. Reading is a skill; you have to do it to get better at it, much like swimming or shooting a basketball.

So, the problem with SSR is that when you get into middle school or high school, it's very easy to start a program like that. But it's very difficult to maintain it. Somebody in the campus needs to kind of carry a flag and come back and remind the faculty repeatedly why we're doing this, why it's important. I do a lot of that with my faculty; I share studies and research that support this idea. It's very clear that the kids who read the most read the best. The kids who read the least read the worst. To me, it is a testing issue but, one of the reasons why SSR programs struggle in a lot of schools is because schools don't particularly do a very good job of making sure kids are surrounded by high interest reading materials.

I've talked with teachers around the country and have often asked them, "When was the last time in a faculty meeting you guys sat around and really had a substantial talk about whether your kids have access to really interesting books?" Sometimes that question gets laughs; we've gotten to a point in school where everything is test, test, test. We don't spend any time as a faculty working with this idea, wrestling with this idea of putting interesting books around our kids.

I believe very strongly that every school should have places on their campus where books flood areas, and not just the library. Of course, the library is super important, but classrooms should also have books in them. If a kid reads a *Goosebumps* book in my classroom and gets interested in this series, then he could go to the library and he could check out ten more of them.

To listen to our entire interview, visit:
www.GettingBoysToRead.com/KellyGallagher

CHAPTER 7:

TRY DIFFERENT TECHNIQUES

When all else fails, try something new! A little creative thinking may be all it takes to inspire him. He may not see, understand, or realize it now, but your dedication and extra effort will pay off for him sooner or later.

TIP # 103

HAVE HIM TRY AUDIO BOOKS

There are thousands of audio books available that can appeal to boys of all ages. When a boy listens to someone else read a book, especially by another male, it can open a world he never knew existed. Not all boys respond the same way, so it pays to know a few pros and cons that accompany audio books.

Pros:

1) Builds Vocabulary

When he is able to hear a difficult word at the same time he sees it, it makes it much easier to recognize that word again in the future. This is especially helpful if a boy has not had much previous exposure to reading.

2) Increases Fluency & Comprehension
As a struggling reader, it's no fun to constantly stumble around a book at a snail's pace. Choppy, interrupted reading takes longer and makes it harder to understand what is happening. Audio books can help alleviate these struggles. They can help him understand what is going on while keeping a smooth flow and quick pace.

3) Modeling
A **GOOD** narrator will eliminate any potential fear, frustration, or pain a boy would experience compared to reading text that is too long or difficult for him to read independently. A good narrator **MODELS** fun and meaningful reading strategies.

Cons:

1) Lack of Availability
Each year, tens of thousands of children's books are published, but the sad reality is that very few ever become available in audio format. When you consider other formats that boys like to read that are readily available – such as magazines, comics, e-reading, and ESPE-CIALLY NONFICTION – audio books seem non-existent.

2) Take Too Long
Many boys don't have much time or patience to listen for extended

periods of time, especially if their bodies are not getting enough movement to compensate for their brains' auditory overload. They are at the mercy of the narrator's speed.

3) Logistical Problems

Listening to audio books is often a tedious and frustrating process. Finding the right title, buying or borrowing it, and then transferring the audio file to a device is usually not very easy. Since there are so many different factors involved, even adults often give up after experiencing technical glitches or obstacles. Smart phones and mobile devices have made the process a lot easier, but they still have a long way to go.

4) Too Boring

Many audio books are not properly narrated – they lack expression and / or fluency. Authors often narrate their own books, even though they may not possess the skills to bring their words to life.

Basic Tips:

- Have him read along in the book while he listens.
- Start him off with shorter audio books.
- While he listens, have him do a simple physical activity like walking, drawing, or fiddling with something in his hands. This will help prevent auditory overload.
- Encourage audio books during car rides.
- Give www.Audible.com a try. The Amazon-based company has over 10,000 titles available for children, including almost 1,000 nonfiction titles.
- Check out audio books for free from your local library. If you need help, bring your laptop and mobile device.

104

USE CAUTION WITH PICTURE BOOKS

As a boy gets older, he may believe the stereotype that picture books are for little kids, especially when he hears adults refer to them as "easy books." Quite often, he worries that if his peers catch him looking at a picture book he will be perceived as:

- a poor reader
- immature
- wimpy

If you force him to read picture books, you risk destroying his overall attitude towards reading. INVITE him through a gentle approach. Suggest that picture books are a great, mature way to examine the thought process of both the author and illustrator – the artistic techniques, elements of writing, and styles of humor.

105 CONNECT READING TO TV SHOWS AND MOVIES

Contrary to the negative impact that TV and movies can have on boys, they can also be effectively used in motivating boys to read.

Find out which TV shows and movies he's into currently and look for related reading materials to extend his background knowledge. For example, if he's obsessed with football, have him research online about his favorite team or player. If he loves watching Animal Planet, have him do a specific search in the Animals section of Amazon's 85,000 children titles.

In many cases, the TV show or movie will publish books to build the brand. For example, an Amazon book search for _Star Wars_ lists over 44,000 results.

TIP # 106

GET MY NEWSLETTER: "BOOKS THAT HOOK"

Teachers and parents are constantly asking me for book suggestions. I've always struggled with this request, because to answer accurately it's important to first know a little background about each boy, specifically these three things:

1. his previous reading experiences (good and bad)
2. his current interests and needs
3. his personality

I have realized that, although every boy has different needs, there are consistencies in the types of topics that a majority of boys are interested in. I spent over a year assembling "Books that Hook," a huge directory of thousands of book suggestions, organized into 100 different "Boy-Focused" categories.

Factors Influencing My Book Suggestions:

- 20 years experience as a teacher-librarian
- Years of library surveys at my schools
- Buying library books for my schools
- Field trips to other libraries, both public and school
- Studying men's TV shows
- Studying popular magazines for boys and men
- Studying advertising directed at boys and men
- Studying gender-based products: clothes, food, drinks, objects, etc.
- Researching articles online
- Formal and informal interviews with boys, educators, and parents
- Analyzing books sold online
- My experience as a guy: "Would I like this?"

This list is available to anyone who signs up for my free email newsletter. Learn more by simply visiting:
www.GettingBoysToRead.com/Newsletter

TIP #

107

Attend The Gurian Summer Institute

E ducators and parents from all over the world come to Colorado each summer to attend a three-day conference called The Gurian Summer Institute. The conference, hosted by famous author Michael Gurian, teaches attendees the key components about gender-based learning.

Visit www.GurianInstitute.com to learn more.

BE PERSISTENT
EVEN WHEN YOU
ARE TIRED

This photo of me was taken after my children asked to go to the library. It had been a long day at work, I wasn't feeling well, and I had tons of things on my mind.

As a parent and educator I empathize with the fact that it's not always easy to put forth the extra effort to help our kids, especially for unappreciative boys who get under our skin.

We can't let that stop us! We need to suck it up, stay positive, and keep fighting for them, especially when they don't seem appreciative. They need us whether they realize it or not.

Like anything in life, determination and hard work will pay off sooner or later – even if it's not visible right away.

Side note: That night I took my kids to the library after all, and they had a great experience.

TIP

109

GET
ADMINISTRATORS
ON BOARD

Principal Deborah Gard

I f you really want to make a big difference, reach out to your administrators for support. Principals, assistant principals, and central office admin have an enormous impact on the attitude and reading performance of boys. They can inspire teachers, parents, and the community to learn more and get involved.

Administrators can help you get reading programs started, fund the purchase of boy-friendly books, pay for author visits, and organize parent literacy nights.

Don't assume your administrator knows about the problems of boys and reading.

Start by scheduling a brief meeting. Share your test data and concerns, and explain some of the things you learned in this book. By reaching out to administrators, you will help the boys whom you care about as well as MANY MORE!

INSPIRE HIS PARENTS (TEACHERS)

As educators, we all know that the most influential teachers throughout a boy's life are his parents. If we truly want to help a struggling boy reader, we must make sure his parents understand a few basic things and then help them stay involved. Unfortunately, most parents lack the proper training, support, and confidence that they need.

Here are 6 Ways to Inspire His Parents:

1. Communicate Often.

Talk with parents often about their sons' reading struggles and successes. Call, email, and use a class or school newsletter to get the word out about how their reading preferences differ from girls'.

2. Provide Information.

There are tons of great books and online articles that can help adults learn about the issues with boys and reading. Encourage parents to read this book, but show them other titles that may also be helpful. Share the great content on my web site, including my free email newsletter – www.GettingBoysToRead.com/Newsletter

3. Remind them to take their sons to the library.

4. Host a Literacy Night.

Give a short 30 minute presentation to his parents, followed by a question-and-answer session. Have book examples on hand as well as a few articles. If possible, provide free babysitting.

5. Give Praise.

Just like boys, parents need to feel positive reinforcement for their efforts – especially dads.

6. Scare Them.

If they're not taking their roles seriously, they may need a more direct approach. With your best, goodhearted intentions, warn them that if they don't get involved now, they will face significantly more problems later on – both in school and in life. If needed, add a dash of guilt.

TIP # 111

FOLLOW MY "QUICK TIPS" ON TWITTER

The majority of Tweets that I post are "Quick Tips" with links to great articles and blog posts. FOLLOW ME at www.Twitter.com/MikeMcQueen

TIP
112

Get Him To Read In The Bathroom

PUT BOOKS HERE

Instead of just letting him sit on the toilet bored while he takes care of business, why not lure him to read? Short books, comics, and magazines are quick reads and fit nicely on the toilet's tank lid. Most guys, of any age, can't resist looking.

TIP

113

USE WRITING TO HELP HIM WITH READING

Writing is a great way to improve reading skills for kids of all ages and ability levels - from preschool through adults. There are many different writing tools and techniques to use; one of these tools is voice recognition technology, a tool that continues to become readily available on cell phones, tablets, and computers.

A teacher asked me for help one day with a tough, struggling teenage boy who suffered from dyslexia. She wanted me to help him find a good book and inspire him to read. I briefly chatted with him about his struggles and then directed him to *A Hole in My Life* by Jack Gantos (a great book for teens, by the way).

The next day, I touched base again with the boy to reconnect and keep his reading momentum going. I encouraged him that the more often he read, the more his reading skills would improve. I emphasized the importance of getting professional reading instruction, but that I had another idea for him to improve his reading skills independently – through WRITING and the use of voice recognition technology.

I sat next to him, pulled out my smartphone, and explained that I have used voice recognition technology for many years. I modeled by recording my voice, READING the dictation to myself (aloud), and then showing him how to edit the errors.

He took his phone out and we found a free dictation App together called Dragon Dictation (there are many others, including ones that are already installed on many devices). We practiced for a little while and then discussed different fun and meaningful ways he could use it in his life, such as text messaging, Facebook, writing notes, and even for school-related assignments. We also discussed how much it could help him in both reading and writing. I wish you could have seen how thankful and appreciative this young man was.

As adults, we must teach our boys that good readers write - often. We need to look for different ways to implement writing, especially in ways that are fun, unpressured, and relevant to their needs. Boys need to see us modeling the writing and reading process we use in our lives.

On a side note, he LOVED the book.

TIP # 114

USE GRAPHIC ORGANIZERS PURPOSEFULLY

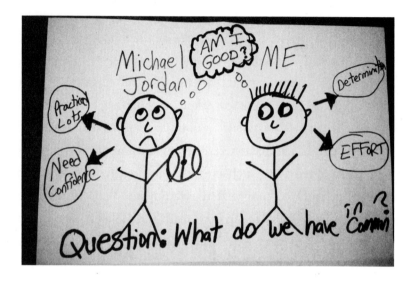

Since boys are more visual by nature, it makes sense to connect them with reading in ways that take advantage of how their brains are wired. If used correctly, graphic organizers can do this. The key is to use graphic organizers in purposeful ways that allow him to:

- Process
- Engage
- Focus
- Interact
- Problem solve

There are many graphic organizer tools available and a very cool variation - an actual visual language called Thinking Maps. Check out www.ThinkingMaps.com and listen to the interview I did with my former principal, Judi Herm - www.GettingBoysToRead.com/JudiHerm

TEACHERS:

Don't slap a graphic organizer worksheet in front of him, focusing only on basic facts that he hopefully remembers from the text. For struggling readers, such assignments and 'busy work' are barriers to success; it's all about helping him to SEE what he reads. Teach him different ways that graphic organizers can be used as tools to HELP him with reading. Have him SHOW you visually what he's thinking - before, during, and/or after he reads. For example, graphic organizers can not only help him record the steps to accomplish a goal, but can help him process WHY those steps are necessary and HOW to solve problems that a text may not cover. You will still obtain the information you need to track his progress, but he will also gain tools to connect with the text on a more personal level.

PARENTS:

Talk with his teachers to gain information about graphic organizers and then do a partner read with an interesting and somewhat challenging book or magazine. During and after you read, just have fun drawing and doodling your thoughts, questions, and feelings about what you read. Model for him by drawing simple stick figures, speech bubbles, labels, and short text. Whatever you do, don't force or pressure him.

INTERVIEW

Interview with Ralph Fletcher, Author of Boy Writers: Reclaiming Their Voices (Stenhouse)

Ralph Fletcher - www.RalphFletcher.com

Below, Mr. Fletcher discusses advice for parents and teachers of reluctant readers/writers.

MIKE MCQUEEN:

What advice would you give parents who have a son who doesn't like to read or write?

RALPH FLETCHER:

- Look for easy, low-pressure occasions (a car ride, vacation) where he might like to write. You might get him an unlined notebook and encourage him to draw (even when he's older).
- You might also suggest he use the notebook as a scrapbook to collect stuff—photos, feathers, ticket stubs, etc. Boys are notorious collectors. This notebook could include weird facts, quotes, rock lyrics, lists, and so forth.
- Show interest in what he writes. If he lets you read it, be there as a reader. If it's funny, laugh. React as a human being. If he doesn't want to share, that's okay.
- Build on strengths. Boys may seem tough, but they want praise—find something specific to celebrate. Don't play teacher. Don't correct his spelling or make any negative comments regarding his handwriting.
- Write something personal and share it with your son. Let him see you writing.

MIKE MCQUEEN:

What are a few important things a TEACHER can do for boys in the classroom?

RALPH FLETCHER:

It's difficult to synthesize a whole book into a few paragraphs; however, here are a few thoughts:

- Just let them write.
- Choice. The boys I surveyed were crying out for more opportunities to write about what they really wanted to.
- Take the long view. Everything we do should be geared to creating life-long writers.

- Look for the humor. If you don't get, or don't accept, boys' quirky humor, they may feel shut off.
- Be more accepting of violent writing (within common sense limits, of course). I know this is a hot issue that makes people nervous, so everyone has to do what feels comfortable in this regard. Note that I said, "more accepting." There should be limits. I personally would allow as much violence in their writings as you would allow in their readings.

To read our entire interview, visit:

http://www.GettingBoysToRead.com/RalphFletcher

Interview with Jeffrey Wilhelm, Co-Author of Reading Don't Fix No Chevys

Dr. Jeffrey Wilhelm - www.JeffreyWilhelm.com

Below, Mr. Wilhelm gives his take on advising parents and teachers of struggling readers.

JEFF WILHELM:

There are so many things to say, but the first thing is to understand that people read for a purpose. No one was ever motivated to read by the cr- blend, but kids will learn the cr-blend and inferring and all kinds of sophisticated strategies in service of doing work. People read to do work, to get things done - whether it's "inner work" - to live through experiences and think about your life, or "outer work" - because you want to do something or go somewhere.

It's really important to tap into pre-existing interests. My daughter likes sports so we have *ESPN Magazine* and *Sports Illustrated for Kids* in the house. There's a book by Scholastic called *The 10 Greatest Hoop Heroes*. I have those things hanging around the house.

One of the things we found was availability. Kids would reach over and grab a book off the table, but they wouldn't walk across the room or go to the library to find it. So make things available to tap into their interests. If you have a family project going on or a family trip planned, have some reading materials available that relates to the project or trip. Be sure to read the material yourself and to talk to your kids about it.

Kids seek relationships, so make the reading relational - make reading something to talk about; make reading a shared interest.

Have a wider view of reading. Boys will say, "I'm not a reader," but I'll say, "Wait a minute, I saw you reading a website about Virginia Tech for about 20 minutes," and he'll say, "Yeah, but I don't do school reading." Have a wider reading net: think of texts more widely as including video games and websites. Construe of reading as including the viewing and use of multimodal texts. Define and name the kids as readers.

There are so many things that we do in school to name kids as non-readers. For example, you got a bad score or you didn't do well on this quiz; we're always naming the deficits, but that's not very motivating -- name what the kids are good at, name what reading can do for them.

To listen to our entire interview, visit:

http://www.GettingBoysToRead.com/JeffreyWilhelm

Index

G

H

I

HAVE MIKE MCQUEEN
SPEAK AT YOUR NEXT EVENT

Mike McQueen is available for keynote presentations, author visits, and educational consulting. He frequently speaks at conferences and loves working with at-risk schools, including those in the "toughest neighborhoods." Mike knows how important it is to be fun, informative, and engaging. His personal and professional stories are inspiring and his use of technology is impressive.

As principal Sharon Ivie put it, "Mike's presentation was **EDUCATIONAL AND LOTS OF FUN!!!** Through the use of his smartphone, he connected students to his work as a 21st century author and reader. He brought 3D characters to life -- popping right out of a book! Students laughed, participated, and could not wait to get their hands on the reading materials he shared. He is an inspiration to all!"

To read more testimonials and schedule a visit from Mike, visit www.MikeMcQueen.com